McCALL'S
BEAUTIFUL
BRUNCH BOOK

McCALL'S
BEAUTIFUL

BRUNCH BOOK

EDITED BY

JEANNE McCLOW

Saturday Review Press
New York

Published simultaneously in Canada by Doubleday Canada Ltd., Toronto.

Library of Congress Catalog Card Number: 75-182484
ISBN 0-8415-0160-2

Saturday Review Press
230 Park Avenue, New York, New York 10017

PRINTED IN THE UNITED STATES OF AMERICA

Design by Margaret F. Plympton

Contents

McCALL'S
BEAUTIFUL
BRUNCH BOOK

Introduction

Nothing is quite so pleasing and satisfying as starting the day off with a fine, stick-to-the-ribs meal. The first meal of the day should be hearty and nutritious enough to provide energy for the activities ahead. As a matter of fact, a leading American nutritionist advises one to "eat breakfast like a king, lunch like a prince, and dinner like a pauper," because the body can best use its food intake in this order. Unfortunately, the pace of daily life has not only cut down on breakfast or even omitted it from the daily menu, but has inverted the ideal order of meals, moving the main meal of the day to evening. Brunch, however, does afford at least an occasional remedy to the modern dilemma of poor eating habits. While it is not the same as breakfast, it includes many high-protein breakfast foods and other foods that are equally nourishing and delicious. Needless to say, brunch can't be served every day; it is generally enjoyed only on weekends when the family and friends can relax with a few extra hours of leisure time. It is, however, nice to know that this delightful meal affords benefits to your body as well as your mind: the relaxed atmosphere of a brunch will give you a psychological lift; the food will nourish your body.

Throughout history, both the size and time of the first meal of the day have varied greatly—from a piece of plain bread to sumptuous, multicourse meals, served at hours ranging from before dawn to well past noon. In fact, the Latin root of the word *dinner* can be translated as "breakfast," perhaps because servants ate breakfast early in the morning, while the English lord broke his fast with dinner around noon.

Although the word *brunch*—a combination of *breakfast* and *lunch*—is a relatively new coinage, there are examples throughout history of meals that closely fit our concept of brunch. The midmorning banquets held by the English nobility, for example, are certainly comparable to the modern brunch. Perhaps the key to a definition of brunch is the word *leisure*. Most Americans, if they eat breakfast at all, have come to regard the meal as purely utilitarian—served early in the morning, made up of a few specific foods—with the sole purpose of filling an empty stomach. Brunch, on the other hand, is a relaxed meal with a varied menu—an extremely pleasurable way to begin the day.

Early American breakfasts, though they usually included some dishes native to the New World, often reflected European culinary preferences. A typical breakfast at Jefferson's Monticello included braised partridge, capitolade of fowl on toast, fried apples, eggs, bacon, cold meats, tansy pudding, hot breads, and battercakes.

In the 1890s, the cookbook *Practical Housekeeping* offered a menu for a six-course summer breakfast for ten. The menu was accompanied by a diagram which showed place settings and positions of a list of eighteen condiments and side dishes. The six courses were melon, fish, chicken with cream gravy, poached eggs on toast, fillets of Porterhouse steak with tomatoes à la mayonnaise, and quartered peaches.

In the late nineteenth and early twentieth centuries, the legendary Diamond Jim Brady began his breakfast with a gallon of orange juice. This was followed by eggs, hominy, muffins, cornbread, chops, flapjacks, fried potatoes, and steak—which lasted him till about eleven-thirty in the morning, at which time he had his midmorning snack of two or three dozen clams and oysters. It is interesting to note that although clams and oysters have for some time been popular as a breakfast dish, in the eighteenth century, Anthelme Brillat-Savarin, author of the classic work on gastronomy *Physiologie du Goût,* was sneered at by contemporary gourmets for his habit of consuming two dozen oysters at breakfast.

During the westward movement in the United States, breakfasts became simple of necessity, the emphasis being placed on quantity. Another well-known figure in the history of American eating, Duncan Hines, claimed that his most memorable gustatory experience was that of a frontier breakfast. After being lost in the wilds between Denver and Cheyenne for three days without food, he rushed into a restaurant in Cheyenne and ordered five dollars' worth of ham and eggs. The proprietor refused, saying that no one could eat that much. To Hines's surprise, one order was more than ample.

The palatial riverboats floating down the Ohio and Mississippi rivers made brunch a popular meal in New Orleans by the turn of the twentieth century. One steamboat captain was so proud of his elaborate brunches that he was said to have ordered his tables laden with foods so that not one inch of tablecloth could be seen.

The invention of the Pullman car in mid-nineteenth century enabled the railroads to compete with the riverboats for comfortable and luxurious traveling. Since food was the main attraction of the boats and trains and the basis of their competition, all meals were incredibly extravagant, and champagne was served in generous quantities. The cost of a champagne breakfast featuring oysters on the half shell, Porterhouse steak, quail, antelope, fresh trout, and terrapin was a mere one dollar. Needless to say, the venture was a money-loser even in those days.

As the United States became more urban, breakfast became a smaller, less important meal. At the present time, most Americans consider bacon or ham and eggs and toast a large breakfast. Although farmers and other manual laborers still eat large morning meals, the white-collar worker, scrambling to make the 7:10 commuter train, has no time for more than a piece of toast or a doughnut and a cup of coffee—if that. Since they are quick to prepare, instant breakfast foods and drinks, packaged cereals, and frozen waffles have recently become enormously popular.

Shortly after World War II, the food freezer, which previously only the wealthy could afford, became a widely owned household appliance. Freezers made seasonal foods available throughout the year; they also made foods that formerly could only be obtained regionally available across the country; and they generally simplified the chores of cooking and shopping. Freezers and other useful appliances, such as electric mixers, electric blenders, and automatic ranges, reduced the need for household and kitchen help. As the practice of hiring servants became rare, American entertaining became less formal and elaborate and more enjoyable.

The speed and efficiency of modern, technological life has given rise to an unprecedented amount of leisure time. Brunch seems to be a natural result of the combination of informality and free time. Paradoxically, though the weekends are becoming longer and freer from household chores, the work-week has become more and more demanding. After a hectic week, rising late and enjoying a relaxed, midmorning brunch is a refreshing way to begin a weekend.

One of the chief assets of brunch is its flexibility. It can be served almost anywhere—in a back yard, on a patio, by a swimming pool, on a porch, on the beach; indoors, it can be served in almost any room of the house—dining room, kitchen, living room, den, recreation room. It can be a sit-down affair, a buffet, or a barbecue; it is adaptable to any climate or occasion. And since brunch is a combination of two very different meals, the number of foods and combinations of dishes are virtually limitless. Shish kebab, grilled tomatoes, and breakfast steaks are just three items that can be cooked on a charcoal grill for an informal outdoor brunch. Quiche tartlets, crêpes, and caviar are good choices for a formal brunch buffet. Many brunch dishes can be prepared in advance, leaving the hostess free to relax and enjoy herself along with her guests. There are no rules governing a brunch: indoor brunches need not necessarily be formal, just as outdoor brunches are not *de rigueur* informal. The style and menu are limited only by the imagination of the hostess or host.

Planning a brunch can be a great deal of fun, and to show you how easy it is, we have included an entire chapter of menus with brunches for all seasons and occasions. These menu plans also include suggestions for attractive serving and imaginative table decor. They are comprised of dishes that combine well and that also result in well-balanced meals. Whether you are planning an informal family gathering or an extra-special buffet with all the fancy trimmings, your brunch can be a memorable occasion. No matter what menu you decide on—one from this book or one of your own devising—you will find that brunch is an easy, elegant, and relaxing way to entertain.

1

COFFEE, TEA, AND
OTHER BEVERAGES

COFFEE

The coffee habit is as American as the word *brunch*. Because the average American consumes nearly three cups of coffee a day, the coffee he drinks should be well made. A pot of perfect coffee is so necessary to every brunch that it deserves special attention here.

Coffee beans were probably a discovery of a ninth-century Ethiopian goatherd who noticed that his goats were unusually lively after munching on some strange green berries. The juice of the berries soon became popular in the Moslem world, where it was known as Islam's wine, honing the mind as wine does, but having none of alcohol's unpleasant side effects.

The Turks, who drank countless thimblefuls of the dark, syrupy liquid, discovered that better coffee was produced when the berries were ground, and they passed the technique on to the European nations, where coffee enjoyed enormous popularity. One of the most important institutions in Europe during the seventeenth century was the coffee house, where artists, writers, and politicians could exchange ideas over steaming mugs of strong coffee.

Preparing the perfect pot of coffee is not difficult, and it is a worthwhile skill to master. The best coffee results from grinding your own beans at home, but if you do not own a grinder, be sure to purchase the proper grind for your coffee maker—regular, drip, fine, or extra fine. Once the coffee, vacuum-packed to retain its freshness, has been opened, keep it in the refrigerator. When you are ready to brew a pot, scrupulously clean and rinse every part of the coffee maker—the oily coffee film that clings to the various parts of your pot will produce bitter coffee. Traces of dish-washing detergent will do the same. For best results, wash your coffee maker in hot water to which baking soda has been added, and scald before using. Purchase a small brush to clean hard-to-get-at spots and use a pipe cleaner to clean the stem.

Always brew as much coffee as your pot will hold. Fill it with fresh cold water, preferably naturally soft water, and place it over medium heat. Electric percolators, of course, regulate the temperature automatically. No matter what type of maker you use, never allow the coffee to boil. Boiling produces bitter, acid-tasting coffee. Use two tablespoons of coffee per cup, and never reuse the grounds.

Following are the three basic methods for making coffee, as well as a description of how to prepare espresso, the full-flavored, strong Italian coffee that is a perfect ending for any meal. If you like the taste of the coffee served in Paris or in New Orleans, add a little ground chicory to the coffee in an eight-cup coffee maker before brewing.

Percolator

Fill the bottom section of an eight-cup percolator with six cups of fresh cold water. Measure one cup regular grind coffee into the basket and place on the stem. Insert the stem into the pot. Over medium heat, percolate the coffee for five minutes, timing from the point when the liquid first shows color. Immediately remove the basket containing the coffee grounds; replace cover.

Drip Coffeepot

Assemble an eight-cup drip coffeepot: Put the coffee section in place. (If using filter paper, insert it before putting in the coffee.) Measure one cup drip grind coffee into the coffee section. Place the water section on top of the coffee section. Pour six cups of boiling water into the water section. Cover; let stand until all the water has dripped through the coffee. Detach the water and coffee sections; discard the grounds; replace the cover.

Vacuum-type Coffee Maker

Fill the lower bowl of an eight-cup vacuum-type coffee maker with six cups of fresh cold water. Attach the upper bowl securely to the lower bowl, adjusting the filter. Measure one cup fine or silex-grind coffee in the upper bowl; cover. Over medium heat, bring the water to boiling (most of the water will rise to the upper bowl). Stir several times; let the coffee maker stand over the heat for about two minutes. Remove from the heat; let the coffee return to the lower bowl. Immediately detach the upper bowl containing the coffee grounds. Cover the coffee.

Caffè Espresso

Use dark-roast Italian coffee, fine grind, with fresh, cold water in a special espresso pot. Follow manufacturer's directions. Serve it hot, in demitasse cups, with a twist of lemon peel in each, if desired.

TEA

While not so popular in the United States as coffee, tea offers a delightful change for an end-of-the-meal beverage. Although its origins are unknown, folklore generally credits its discovery to the Indian founder of Zen Buddhism, who had come to China several centuries after Christ to preach his philosophy. Teahouses were firmly established institutions in China by the eighth century.

The Japanese also grew to love the beverage and developed an elaborate ritual regarding its proper service. Invitations and replies, the proper attire, and the actual drinking of the liquid were all precisely prescribed. Even today, tea-service schools can be found all over Japan.

The custom of afternoon tea, served from a tray laden with little sandwiches and cakes, was established in England about the mid-nineteenth century, to stave off the hunger pangs that resulted from the long interlude between breakfast and dinner. Since that time, tea has been the national drink of England. It was formerly as popular in the English colonies, but the consumption of tea has, for some reason, declined rapidly in the United States.

If you wish to offer your brunch guests a change of pace, prepare a pot of freshly brewed tea.

First, choose a tea that best suits your taste. Although there is only one kind of tea plant, there are several varieties of tea marketed; these are the results of differing factors such as climate, age, method of drying, and blending. The tea leaves are systematically graded according to their age. The three basic kinds of tea are black, green, and oolong. Green tea is the most astringent; black is the least. Orange pekoe, made from the youngest leaves, is considered the best.

To make a tea concentrate, bring three cups of naturally soft, cold water to a boil in a glass or enameled pot. The moment the water reaches a brisk boil, drop in two-thirds of a cup of tea leaves, remove from the heat, and cover it. Allow the tea to steep in the pot for three to five minutes before straining it into a teapot. Have a second teapot of very hot water ready. Pour one or two tablespoons of concentrate into each teacup and fill with hot water. This concentrate will make about twenty-five cups.

Place sugar cubes and thin lemon slices on a tray to pass to your guests. A jigger of rum will further enhance the tea. If you wish to follow English custom, offer cold milk instead of lemon. By adding ice to the diluted tea and garnishing the glasses with mint sprigs and lemon, you will have prepared an excellent iced tea.

Because of the high caffeine content of tea and coffee, herbal brews have recently regained the tremendous appeal they held in the past. Try steeping the leaves of such herbs as mint, thyme, sage, lemon verbena; the bark of sassafras; rose hips; the flowers of hibiscus, linden, orange, and wintergreen; and the seeds of fennel. You can grow many of them in pots on your windowsill or in your garden. Dried forms are now available in gourmet and health food stores. Depending on the strength of the herb, allow from one-quarter to one teaspoon dried herbs or from one-half to two tablespoons fresh herbs per cup. Steep in a nonmetal pot for three to ten minutes in water which has first been brought to a brisk boil. Strain and serve with honey or lemon.

OTHER BEVERAGES

Because all beverages, whether alcoholic or nonalcoholic, are intrinsic to any brunch, this section deals with the preparation and service of all sorts of drinks. A number of milk-based drinks have, for instance, been included since brunch is often a family affair. On those occasions, though, that are not family gatherings, you may wish to serve your beverage before the guests are seated as well as during the meal; in this way, everyone can become acquainted or reestablish friendships informally before they sit down at the table.

Punches are very practical for brunch because they relieve the host or hostess of bartending duties and because they are appealing to the eye as well as to the taste. An attractive punch bowl and ladle are, of course, essential, and be sure to have plenty of cups on hand. If you don't have a punch bowl, improvise—a good improvisation is often the longest-remembered aspect of a party. You might use a large, solid-bottomed ceramic flower pot, a huge glass martini pitcher, an antique copper or cast-iron cooking pot, or you might funnel the punch into interesting wine bottles you have collected. The bright enameled Scandinavian ladles are readily available, inexpensive, and quite cheerful.

In making a punch, use either fresh juices or frozen concentrates—canned juices vary too much in flavor to be dependable. After mixing them, allow them time to blend—about one hour—or to chill, if necessary, before adding soda or water. If you don't wish to ice the punch with a decorative ring or mold, use ice blocks that have been frozen in the ice trays without their cube separators.

If, however, you would like to make an ice ring, here's how to do it. Run the amount of water to be frozen into a bowl and chill until very cold. Stir several times to eliminate the bubbles. Choose a metal mold that is either ring- or tube-shaped. Make sure that you have on hand whatever decorative fruits and leaves you are planning to use—green and red maraschino cherries; lemon, lime, and orange slices; mint sprigs; clusters of grapes; whole fresh cherries and strawberries; and some glossy, perfect leaves, perhaps grape leaves. To begin, partially freeze a layer of the reserved or chilled water in the mold. Remove from the freezer and arrange a layer of fruits and leaves on it. Then carefully pour over it another layer of cold water. Partially freeze, decorate again; and pour remaining water over it if the depth of the mold permits. When ready to unmold, wrap a hot, wet towel around the mold and turn it upside down into the punch. A word of caution: Be selective in the use of fruit—a punch bowl that is too elaborate merely looks crowded.

Besides the dozens of punch recipes given in this book, there are many others that you can make in your blender by experimenting with different fruit combinations. Remember that a squeeze of lemon juice will normally do away with any unpleasing gray color that may result. If these drinks are to be served in individual glasses, garnish the glasses with greenery—fresh mint or sweet woodruff or whatever small leaves you like. Or you may decorate with maraschino cherries, pineapple chunks, orange or lemon slices, strawberries, or combinations of these speared on a toothpick. If you want to add only a slight alcoholic taste to a fruit drink, add one or two tablespoons of sherry, bourbon, or other whiskey to the water in an ice tray. The cubes will flavor the drink but will not interfere with the taste of the food to come.

Unless you are serving wine with your brunch, you can serve your punch throughout the meal as well as before. Just be sure not to make it so potent that it will overpower the flavors of your foods.

Wine, of course, is a perfect accompaniment to any brunch. Whether you choose a red, white, or a rosé, wine is an extremely sociable drink which sharpens the mind and stimulates conversation. Or you may decide on any of the popular beers or ales, particularly suitable to outdoor brunches. Light or dark, imported or domestic, these beverages are great favorites as brunch accompaniments.

NONALCOHOLIC BEVERAGES

SUMMER ICED COFFEE

½ cup instant coffee	2 trays ice cubes
¾ teaspoon cinnamon	6 twists lemon peel
⅛ teaspoon cloves	
1 cup boiling water	Sugar and cream (optional)

1. Combine coffee, cinnamon, and cloves in a 1-quart measure. Add boiling water; stir until coffee mixture is dissolved.

2. Add 3 cups cold water; refrigerate, covered, until ready to serve.

3. To serve: Fill 6 tall glasses with ice cubes. Place a lemon twist in each; fill with chilled coffee. Serve with sugar and cream, if desired.

Makes 6 servings.

VIENNESE COFFEE

½ cup heavy cream
1 tablespoon confectioners' sugar
½ teaspoon vanilla extract

3 cups hot extra-strong coffee
½ teaspoon grated orange peel
4 (1½-inch) cinnamon sticks

1. Combine cream, sugar, and vanilla; with rotary beater, beat until stiff.

2. Pour coffee into 4 cups. Float whipped cream mixture on top.

3. Garnish cream with orange peel, and place cinnamon stick in each cup. Serve at once.

Makes 4 servings.

PEACH- OR STRAWBERRY-FLAVORED MILK

1 package (10 ounces) frozen peaches or strawberries

2 cups milk

1. Thaw peaches or strawberries according to package directions. Turn into blender container.

2. Add milk; cover; blend, at low or medium speed, a few seconds, or just until blended. Or beat together in medium-size bowl, with electric mixer at high speed.

3. Chill very well, and serve.

Makes 3 cups.

PEPPERMINT-CHOCOLATE MILK

1 quart milk	6 peppermint-candy sticks
4 envelopes (¾-ounce size) chocolate-flavor milk-shake mix	Marshmallow topping

1. In electric-blender container, combine 2 cups milk and 2 envelopes milk-shake mix. Blend at high speed 10 seconds. Repeat with remaining milk and mix.
2. To serve: Pour into 6 (8-ounce) glasses. Place a candy stick in each, and top with a generous spoonful of topping.
Makes 6 servings.

RASPBERRY-FLAVORED MILK

1 package (10 ounces) frozen raspberries	3 cups milk

1. Thaw raspberries according to package directions. Turn into blender container.
2. Add milk; cover; blend, at low or medium speed, a few seconds, or just until blended. Or beat together in medium-size bowl, with electric mixer at high speed.
3. Chill very well, and serve.
Makes 4 cups.

HOT MULLED CIDER

2 quarts cider	24 whole cloves
½ cup sugar	4 (4-inch) cinnamon sticks
Dash salt	16 whole allspice

1. Combine all ingredients in large pan. Bring to boil, stirring until sugar is dissolved.
2. Cool. Refrigerate, covered, several hours.

3. Just before serving, reheat slowly. Strain to remove spices. Serve hot, in mugs or punch cups.
Makes 16 (4-ounce) servings.

FRESH LEMONADE

3 lemons
¾ cup fine granulated sugar

Ice cubes

Mint sprigs

1. Wash lemons well. With sharp knife, slice crosswise into very thin slices.
2. Discard end slices and seeds. Put lemon slices in bottom of large bowl or sturdy pitcher. Add sugar.
3. With potato masher or wooden spoon, pound lemon slices until they are broken and sugar is dissolved.
4. Add 1 tray of ice cubes and 2 cups cold water. Stir until very cold.
5. To serve: Pour lemonade, with lemon slices, over ice cubes in tall glasses. Garnish each with a mint sprig.
Makes 2 to 4 servings.

LEMON-AND-LIME MIST

½ cup lemon juice
¼ cup lime juice
⅔ cup granulated sugar
1¼ cups chilled club soda

½ cup chopped ice

Tropical flowers

1. In electric blender, combine juices, sugar, soda, and ice.
2. Blend at high speed, covered, ½ minute.
3. Pour into chilled glasses; garnish each with flower.
Makes 6 (3-ounce) servings.

Daiquiris
Reduce sugar to ¼ cup. Omit soda; add 1¼ cups white rum to fruit juices before blending.
Makes 8 (3-ounce) servings.

BREAKFAST ORANGE BLOSSOMS

1 can (12 ounces) frozen
orange-juice concentrate
1 can (12 ounces) apricot
nectar
2 tablespoons grenadine

¼ teaspoon angostura bitters

Ice cubes
3 orange slices, quartered
12 maraschino cherries with
stems

1. In large pitcher, reconstitute frozen orange juice as label directs. Stir in apricot nectar, grenadine, and bitters.
2. Pour over ice in old-fashioned glasses. Garnish each with quarter of orange slice and cherry, fastened together with fancy wooden pick. Serve with short straws.
Makes 12 servings.

ORANGE JULEP

1 can (1 pint, 2 ounces)
orange-apricot juice
2 tablespoons lemon juice

Fresh mint

Ice cubes (optional)

1. In large pitcher, combine orange-apricot juice, lemon juice, and 1 tablespoon chopped mint.
2. Chill overnight.
3. Serve in small glasses. Decorate each with a sprig of mint. Serve over ice, if desired.
Makes 6 servings.

ORANGE-PINEAPPLE SPRITZERS

1 can (6 ounces) frozen
orange-juice concentrate
1 can (6 ounces) frozen
pineapple-juice concentrate
1 bottle (7 ounces) club soda,
chilled

¼ teaspoon angostura bitters

Crushed ice

1. Mix frozen juices with 3½ cups water. Add club soda and bitters.
2. Pour over ice in old-fashioned glasses.
Makes 6 servings.

FRUIT PUNCH

1 can (6 ounces) frozen
   pink-lemonade concentrate
1 can (6 ounces) frozen
   lemonade concentrate
1 can (6 ounces) frozen limeade
   concentrate

Yellow and green food coloring
2 bottles (1-pint, 12-ounce size)
   ginger ale, chilled

1. In separate bowls, combine each can of concentrate with 2 cups water.
2. Tint plain lemonade with 1 drop yellow food coloring; tint limeade with 1 drop green food coloring.
3. Pour mixtures into separate ice-cube trays, to make cubes; freeze 3 to 3½ hours, or until firm.
4. To serve: Turn ice cubes into a large punch bowl. Add ginger ale; mix gently. Let stand 10 minutes.
Makes about 25 servings, 6 ounces each.

PINEAPPLE SWIZZLES

2 cans (1-pint, 2-ounce size)
   unsweetened pineapple juice
2 cans (6-ounce size) thawed
   frozen orange-juice
   concentrate, undiluted
¼ cup lime juice

12 drops angostura bitters
1 jar (8 ounces) maraschino
   cherries

Mint sprigs
Pineapple chunks

1. In large drink shaker or bowl, combine pineapple juice and orange-juice concentrate, mixing well.
2. Add lime juice, bitters, and 3 tablespoons cherry juice; mix well.
3. Refrigerate until well chilled—several hours.

4. Shake well just before serving.

5. Pour into tall glasses; garnish each with a cherry, mint sprig, and pineapple chunk on a drinking straw.

Makes 6 (8-ounce) servings.

Note: To make frosted edge on glasses, dip rim of each in fruit juice, then in granulated sugar to coat well. Refrigerate glasses until well chilled.

Rum Swizzles

Add 2 cups white rum to chilled juice mixture; shake well just before serving.

Makes 8 (8-ounce) servings.

STRAWBERRY COOLER

1 cup pineapple juice	½ cup sugar
1 orange, peeled, seeded, and cut	12 strawberries
½ lemon, peeled, seeded, and cut	Ice cubes (optional)
	1 quart ginger ale (optional)

1. Place pineapple juice, orange, lemon, sugar, and strawberries in blender container.

2. Blend at high speed, covered, 30 seconds, or until smooth.

3. Serve as milk-shake-type drink; makes 2 large servings. Or pour into punch bowl over ice, and add 1 quart ginger ale.

Makes 12 (4-ounce size) servings.

STRAWBERRY-LEMONADE PUNCH

2 cans (6-ounce size) frozen pink-lemonade concentrate, undiluted	1 package (10 ounces) frozen sliced strawberries
1 can (6 ounces) frozen orange-juice concentrate, undiluted	1 bottle (1 pint, 12 ounces) ginger ale, chilled

1. In punch bowl, combine pink lemonade, orange juice, straw-berries, and 3 cups water. Refrigerate.
2. To serve: Pour ginger ale into juice mixture in bowl; stir well. Makes 2½ quarts.

TOMATO-ORANGE JUICE ON THE ROCKS

2 cups orange juice
1 cup tomato juice

Ice cubes

Lemon slices (optional)

1. Combine orange and tomato juices in large pitcher; mix well. Refrigerate until well chilled—overnight.
2. To serve: Stir to mix well. Pour over ice in small glasses. Decorate with a slice of lemon, if you wish.
Makes 6 servings.

ORANGE NOG

1¾ cups milk
2 eggs

¼ cup orange-flavored instant
   breakfast drink

1. Combine all ingredients in medium-size bowl.
2. Beat, with rotary beater, until frothy and well blended.
Makes about 2½ cups; 2 servings.

ALCOHOLIC BEVERAGES

CAFÉ BRÛLOT

2 (1½-inch) cinnamon sticks
2 whole cloves
¼ teaspoon grated nutmeg
¼ teaspoon whole allspice
Peel of 1 small orange, removed
   in a spiral

1 lemon slice
12 sugar cubes
1 cup cognac
5 cups hot strong coffee

1. In chafing dish, over direct heat, combine all ingredients except coffee. Heat until hot throughout—about 10 minutes.

2. In heated ladle, ignite a little of the hot cognac mixture. Then pour back into the cognac mixture in chafing dish.

3. While cognac is flaming, pour in hot coffee. Serve in brûlot or demitasse cups.

Makes 12 servings.

Note: Coffee made from dark-roast Italian coffee, fine grind, in a special caffè-espresso pot is preferred. Follow manufacturer's directions for making.

IRISH COFFEE

4 tablespoons sugar	8 cups hot strong black coffee
1 cup Irish whiskey	1 cup chilled whipped cream

1. Place 1½ teaspoons sugar into each of 8 (7-ounce) goblets.

2. Add 1 ounce whiskey to each. Fill with coffee to within ½ inch of rims.

3. Float a heaping tablespoon of whipped cream on top of each goblet by sliding it off a spoon onto coffee.

4. Serve at once.

Makes 8 servings.

MILK PUNCH

1½ cups bourbon or brandy	½ cup heavy cream
1½ pints dairy half-and-half	Nutmeg
1 teaspoon vanilla extract	
2½ tablespoons confectioners' sugar	Crushed ice (optional)

1. Combine bourbon, half-and-half, and vanilla. Stir in sugar until dissolved. Cover; refrigerate several hours, or until very well chilled.

2. Just before serving, whip cream until stiff. Pour bourbon mixture into punch bowl or glass serving bowl. Set bowl in a bowl of crushed ice, if desired.

3. Spoon whipped cream on punch. Sprinkle with freshly grated nutmeg.

Makes 8 or 9 (punch-cup) servings.

FROSTY DAIQUIRI PUNCH

Fern Ice Block (see below)
Frosted Punch Bowl (see p. 20)
1 bottle (16 ounces) daiquiri
   mix
6 tablespoons superfine sugar

2½ cups light rum
½ cup curaçao or cointreau
2 dozen ice cubes
1 bottle (1 pint, 12 ounces)
   club soda, chilled

1. Day ahead, prepare Fern Ice Block and Frosted Punch Bowl.

2. In pitcher or bowl, combine daiquiri mix and sugar, and stir until sugar is dissolved. Add rum and curaçao.

3. Refrigerate, stirring occasionally, until well chilled—about 3 hours.

4. To serve: Place Fern Ice Block in Frosted Punch Bowl. Place half of daiquiri mixture and 1 dozen ice cubes in electric blender; blend, at high speed, 15 to 20 seconds. Pour into punch bowl. Repeat with remaining mixture and ice. Stir in club soda.

Makes about 20 (4-ounce) servings.

Note: You may use 2 (6-ounce size) cans frozen daiquiri mix. If blender is not available, crush ice cubes very fine. Place with daiquiri mixture in jar with tight-fitting lid. Shake vigorously 1 minute.

FERN ICE BLOCK

1. Day before using, make Ice Block: Pour 2 cups cold water into a 2½-quart bowl. Freeze until thin coating of ice forms on top—about 2 hours.

2. Meanwhile, wash 5 fern tips and trim to 5 inches long. Also, wash 1 bunch (1½ pounds) green grapes. Break ice in bowl, and arrange ferns against side of bowl, tip ends up. Arrange grapes in center.

3. Place in freezer until grapes and water are frozen. Then fill bowl with water. Freeze overnight.

4. To unmold: Dip bowl in warm water until ice loosens. Turn out on waxed paper. Return to freezer if not using at once.

FROSTED PUNCH BOWL

1. Beat 1 egg white with 1 tablespoon water. Use to brush a band about 1½ inches wide on outside of punch bowl, at top.

2. Sprinkle sheet of waxed paper with granulated sugar. Roll edge of bowl in sugar, to frost it.

3. Let stand at room temperature about 20 minutes; then roll in sugar again.

4. Set aside to dry—3 to 4 hours or overnight.

PIÑA COLADAS

½ cup cream of coconut
1 cup unsweetened pineapple
   juice, chilled
⅔ cup light rum

2 cups crushed ice

Pineapple spears (optional)

1. Refrigerate 6 cocktail glasses, to chill well—about 1 hour.

2. In electric blender, combine the cream of coconut, pineapple juice, rum, and ice; cover, and blend at high speed ½ minute.

3. Pour into chilled glasses. If desired, serve with a pineapple spear in each glass.

Makes 6 servings.

Note: Cream of coconut may be purchased as a 1-pound can of coconut-milk cream.

PLANTER'S PUNCH

1 cup lime juice
1 cup orange juice

1 cup dark rum
1 cup granulated sugar

1 jar (8 ounces) maraschino
  cherries
8 dashes angostura bitters

1 tray ice cubes

Orange and lime slices

1. In blender or drink shaker, combine lime juice, orange juice, rum, sugar, 1½ teaspoons maraschino-cherry juice, and bitters.
2. Blend, at low speed, or shake 1 minute. Pour over ice cubes in pitcher; stir well. Let stand 10 minutes.
3. Strain into chilled glasses or small ceramic coconut shells.
4. Garnish each with cherry, orange slice, and lime slice speared on fancy pick.

Makes about 6 (6-ounce size) servings.

RUM SWIZZLES

6 cups grapefruit juice
3 cups orange juice
1 quart cider
12 whole cloves
2 (2-inch) pieces cinnamon
  stick
2 cups grenadine
1 to 2 cups light rum

3 or 4 drops angostura bitters
8 drops red food coloring

Cinnamon sticks (optional)
Orange slices stuck with cloves
  (optional)
Ice cubes (optional)

1. In 6-quart saucepan, combine grapefruit juice, orange juice, cider, cloves, and cinnamon stick. Bring to boil; reduce heat, and simmer, covered, 30 minutes. Strain to remove spices.
2. Return mixture to large saucepan. Stir in grenadine, rum, bitters, and food coloring; mix well.
3. To serve hot, bring to boil, covered. If desired, garnish each serving with a cinnamon stick and orange slice.
4. To serve cold, serve in chilled punch bowl over ice cubes. If desired, float orange slices stuck with cloves on top.
5. Keep chilled in refrigerator.

Makes about 4 quarts.

Note: Very good as a nonalcoholic punch, too, if you wish to omit rum.

RUM-TEA PUNCH

1 can (6 ounces) frozen
lemonade concentrate,
undiluted
½ cup superfine sugar
¼ cup instant tea
¾ cup light rum

¼ cup brandy
1 lemon, thinly sliced

Ice cubes
Fresh mint sprigs

1. In large bowl, combine undiluted lemonade concentrate, 4 cups cold water, the sugar, and tea. Stir until concentrate is melted and sugar is dissolved.

2. Add rum, brandy, and lemon slices. Pour over ice cubes in punch bowl. Garnish with mint.

Makes 12 (punch-cup) servings.

MARGARITAS

½ cup lemon juice
Coarse salt
1 cup plus 2 tablespoons
tequila

⅓ cup cointreau
¼ cup superfine sugar
2 cups cracked ice

1. Before squeezing lemons for juice, twirl rims of 8 cocktail glasses on cut lemon surface. Then dip rims of glasses in salt. Refrigerate glasses about 1 hour.

2. Combine lemon juice, tequila, cointreau, sugar, and ice in electric blender; cover, and blend at high speed ½ minute.

3. Pour into chilled glasses.

Makes 8 servings.

Note: Or use a margarita-cocktail mix. Some have all the necessary ingredients and are ready for serving. Others just require the tequila.

ORANGE BLOSSOMS

3 cups orange juice
½ cup lemon juice
½ cup grenadine
1 bottle (¾ quart) martini
   cocktail, chilled

1 bottle (1 pint, 12 ounces)
   club soda, chilled

Ice cubes

1. In large pitcher or bowl, combine orange juice, lemon juice, and grenadine; stir until well blended. Refrigerate until well chilled—several hours.
2. To serve: Add martini cocktail and club soda to fruit-juice mixture; mix well. Pour over ice in old-fashioned glasses.
Makes about 20 (4-ounce) servings.

BLOODY MARYS

1 can (1 quart) tomato juice,
   well chilled
1 cup vodka
1 teaspoon Worcestershire
   sauce

2 tablespoons lemon juice
1 teaspoon celery salt
1 teaspoon salt
Few drops Tabasco

1. In large pitcher, combine tomato juice with rest of ingredients.
2. Stir to mix well.
Makes 1 quart.

VODKA WASSAIL BOWL

Whole cloves
3 large oranges
1 gallon apple juice
½ cup lemon juice

10 (2-inch) cinnamon sticks
 2 cups vodka
 ¼ cup brandy

1. Preheat oven to 350°F.
2. Insert cloves, ½ inch apart, in unpeeled oranges. Place in shallow pan; bake, uncovered, 30 minutes.
3. Meanwhile, heat apple juice in large kettle until bubbles form around edge of kettle.
4. Add lemon juice, cinnamon sticks, and baked oranges. Heat, covered, over low heat, 30 minutes. Remove from heat.
5. Add vodka and brandy; mix well. Pour into punch bowl. Serve warm.

Makes about 36 (4-ounce) servings.

WHISKEY-SOUR PUNCH

1 can (6 ounces) frozen orange-juice concentrate, undiluted
1 can (6 ounces) frozen lemon-juice concentrate, undiluted
1 tablespoon angostura bitters
2 tablespoons sugar
1 jar (8 ounces) maraschino cherries

1 bottle (¾ quart) whiskey-sour cocktail, chilled
1 bottle (1 pint, 12 ounces) club soda, chilled

Ice Block (see p. 25)

1 large navel orange, thinly sliced
1 lemon, thinly sliced

1. In pitcher or bowl, combine frozen fruit-juice concentrates, bitters, sugar, and syrup drained from maraschino cherries. When juices are thawed, stir until well blended. Refrigerate, with cherries, until well chilled—several hours or overnight.
2. To serve: In punch bowl, combine fruit-juice mixture, whiskey-sour cocktail, and club soda; mix well.
3. Float Ice Block in punch. Place cherries and orange and lemon slices around ice.

Makes about 18 (4-ounce) servings.

ICE BLOCK

Day before using, make Ice Block: Fill a bowl with 2 quarts water, and let stand at room temperature 1 hour. Stir occasionally to release air bubbles. Mound 2 trayfuls of ice cubes in a 2-quart, fancy round mold; fill with the water. Freeze until firm. To unmold: Dip mold in warm water until ice loosens; turn out on waxed paper. Return to freezer if not using at once.

GLÖGG

1⅔ cups cognac	4 (3-inch) cinnamon sticks
1 bottle (⅘ quart) red wine	1 cup sugar
1 bottle (⅘ quart) port	
18 whole cloves	1 cup golden raisins
1 nutmeg, crushed	1 cup blanched almonds

1. Combine all ingredients, reserving some raisins and almonds, in large saucepan; heat, stirring, over medium heat, just until vapor starts to rise.
2. Ignite; stir until sugar is dissolved. Heat, stirring, 10 minutes. (Do not boil.)
3. Ladle the Glögg immediately into punch cups, spooning some raisins and blanched almonds into each cup.
Makes 12 to 14 servings.

ROSÉ-WINE SPRITZER

1 bottle (⅘ quart) rosé wine, chilled	Ice cubes
1 bottle (12 ounces) club soda, chilled	

1. Pour wine and soda into large pitcher; stir just to combine. Add ice cubes.
2. Serve in chilled wineglasses.
Makes about 8 (6-ounce) servings.

SANGRÍA

1 bottle (1 pint, 7 ounces) red
  Spanish wine
2 tablespoons sugar
1 lemon, sliced
½ orange, sliced

2 ounces cointreau
2 ounces Spanish brandy
1 bottle (12 ounces) club soda,
  chilled
24 ice cubes

1. In large pitcher, combine wine, sugar, and lemon and orange slices. Stir until sugar is dissolved. Stir in cointreau, brandy, club soda, and ice cubes.

2. Let stand 15 to 20 minutes.

Makes 6 servings.

CHAMPAGNE PUNCH BOWL

1 large bunch seedless green
  grapes (about 1½ pounds)
2 cups sauterne
1 cup cognac
2 tablespoons sugar
2 bottles (7-ounce size) club
  soda, chilled

6 strawberries, hulls on, washed
  (optional)
1 bottle (⅘ quart) champagne,
  chilled

1. Day ahead: Wash grapes; place on small tray. Place in freezer.

2. Several hours before serving: In pitcher or bowl, combine sauterne, cognac, and sugar; stir until sugar is dissolved. Refrigerate.

3. To serve: Pour sauterne mixture into punch bowl. Stir in soda. Add frozen grapes and the strawberries.

4. Pour champagne into punch just before serving.

Makes about 16 (4-ounce) servings.

2

FRUIT

Flavorful, nutritious fruit, served either at the beginning or at the end of a meal, is a natural for brunches. From a nutritional standpoint, fruit is the perfect way to begin every day since it is an excellent energy producer and supplies large amounts of natural vitamin C.

Fresh fruit is always more flavorful than the canned or frozen varieties; visit your grocery or the fruit market to make your selections, and remember the following hints about storing fruit. If they are still on the green side, allow the fruit to ripen in a dark place at room temperature. Avoid packing them so closely that they touch, and do not bruise them. Once they have ripened, refrigerate them. Do not wash them until you are ready to serve them, and then rinse them under cold water very quickly in order to preserve their flavor and vitamins. When cutting fruit, use a stainless steel knife to avoid discoloration. A little lemon juice added to cut fruit will retard darkening caused by contact with the air.

You may incorporate fruit into a brunch menu in many ways. Small berries may be served whole in a pretty fruit bowl with a sprinkle of granulated or confectioners' sugar, and cream or sour cream may be served with them, if you wish. Large fruits may be sliced or cubed, topped with sugar, and drizzled with lime or lemon juice, sherry, or port. You may also mix fruits according to taste, and include some canned or frozen varieties with the fresh fruit. A delicious way to serve mixed fruit is to prick each piece with a fork and marinate the fruit in a wine or liquor—sherry, marsala, kirsch, port, rum, and brandy are all good choices. Such dishes may either be chilled or served at room temperature and flambéed. They make delightful brunch desserts, particularly when accompanied by scoops of lime or lemon sherbet or slices of freshly made poundcake.

Fruits that have been poached will be a welcome part of any winter brunch. To prepare poached fruits, simply drop them into a pot of boiling water or fruit juice, reduce the heat at once, and simmer only until tender. Drain and add sugar if desired. Mix several different kinds of poached fruit to accompany a meat platter or serve as an appetizer in attractive bowls. Try baking fruit at 350°F. until tender, basting frequently, if cooked uncovered. When the fruit is almost cooked, fill with a tart jelly or blue cheese and return to the oven for another ten minutes. This dish makes an interesting accompaniment to a meat course.

All fruit preparations should be attractively served and garnished. Gracefully shaped sherbet glasses are a good choice for individual servings, since they allow the colors and shapes of the fruit to be seen. Layer the fruit in each cup for a lovely visual effect. For a common-serving dish use a large crystal bowl or brandy snifter. Mint sprigs are always a popular garnish, but many other types of greenery may be used. Strawberries or cherries also make good toppings.

Of course, fruit may be served fresh, without any preparation at all. One of the best endings to a brunch is a platter of beautiful polished apples surrounded by wedges of cheese—Gouda, Brie, Camembert, Liederkranz, Roquefort, Muenster, Port du Salut, or Bel Paese. Cheeses should be at room temperature. Remove them from the refrigerator at least an hour before serving. Firm juicy apples are best for dessert platters; Delicious apples are the most popular. All types of melons, pears, and grapes go equally well with these cheeses. If you wish, serve slices of pumpernickel bread, cocktail crackers, or nuts.

Fruits also make wonderful table decorations. A very ripe pineapple provides a beautiful centerpiece. Slice off the top and bottom and set them aside; cut out the insides within about one-half inch of the edge, slice the fruit into wedges, and place the wedges inside the pineapple to be eaten at the end of a meal. Replace the leafy top and surround the pineapple with fresh cherries, strawberries, or flowers to achieve the full dramatic effect. This section and the menu section include instructions for other centerpieces using fruits; melons are particularly suitable for this purpose.

Berries and cherries should be selected on the basis of good color, and should not be washed until immediately before serving. Wash blueberries, blackberries, and huckleberries in a bowl, discarding those that rise to the top. Keep them in the refrigerator loosely packed in a covered container.

The many varieties of *melons* now available are especially well-suited to brunches. Their light color, fragrance, and flavor are particularly refreshing in the morning. It is difficult to learn how to select a good melon, but it may help you to remember that a ripe melon will yield to pressure applied to its stem end. Vine-ripened fruit is, by far, preferable to store- or home-ripened; a sunken, calloused stem end indicates that a melon is vine-ripened.

Ripe *cantaloupe* should have a sweet, musky aroma, and the veins on its rind should be well raised. *Persian melons* and *cranshaws,* relatives of the cantaloupe, follow the same rule. *Honeydews* should have smooth creamy white or yellow skins. A yellow skin and deep ridges indicate that a *casaba* is ripe. *Watermelon* should yield a thin green rind when you scrape it with your fingernail. Or use the old-fashioned test of thumping it: it should respond with a heavy full sound. Store all melons at room temperature, out of direct sunlight, and chill only before serving. Once cut, exposed melon should be covered.

The *avocado,* also called the alligator pear, is found in many forms, ranging from a small, round shiny green ball to a larger, deep brown pear shape. Because these fruits ripen at different times in different parts of the country, they are available the year around. If ripe, they will be heavy for their size and yield to slight pressure. The color should be uniform and the shell should be unmarred. If still firm, ripen them at home at room temperature and then refrigerate before serving.

Apples are wonderful for use in fruit dishes as well as for eating fresh, perhaps with cheese. They should be firm, well-shaped, and unblemished. The best eating varieties are Gravenstein, Wealthy, McIntosh, both Golden and Red Delicious, Yellow Transparent, Grimes Golden, Jonathan, Stayman, Winesap, Northern Spy, and Baldwin. Store small amounts in a plastic bag in the refrigerator; larger amounts should be kept in a cool, dark, well-ventilated place and sorted through occasionally to remove decaying ones.

The *apricot* allegedly brings both good health and longevity. Difficult to store and even more difficult to grow, the fruits should be kept in a covered container or in a perforated plastic bag in the refrigerator. Choose plump, fairly firm fruit that is uniform in color.

The *bananas* we eat are all imported. Plantains, a starchier relative of the familiar yellow banana, must be cooked because of their fibrous quality. Ripe bananas are slightly soft to the touch and yellow, mottled with brown. Once bananas are ripe, they may be refrigerated to prevent further ripening, although refrigeration will turn the skins brown. If not mature enough to eat, keep them at room temperature in a closed paper bag until they reach the desired color. For best results, bananas should be ripened at home.

Oranges were formerly a luxury that only the very rich could afford, but today they are inexpensive and appear on most family tables every day as fruit or juice. Temples and Valencias, mainly from Florida, are the juice oranges, and the navels from California are for eating. Look for oranges that are thin-skinned, firm, and heavy. Coarse skins and puffiness indicate dry fruit. Color is not an indication of ripeness, since most of our oranges are processed to achieve their rich orange hue. Always keep oranges refrigerated; once picked they cannot ripen further. *Tangerines* and *tangelos,* a cross between an orange and a grapefruit, are also delicious.

Grapefruit, so called because the fruit occasionally appears on a tree in grapelike clusters, has been scientifically improved and sweetened in recent years. Like oranges, grapefruits are high in vitamin C. There are several varieties available. The pink—a natural color—is sometimes more expensive than the white. Seedless types are most popular, although this designation simply means that fewer than five seeds are present. As with oranges, look for thin skins, uniform shapes, and heavy weight. Discolorations of skin are not necessarily indications of poor quality. Keep grapefruit refrigerated.

Both *lemons* and *limes* are perfect as garnishes and flavorings in cooking. They should be selected on the same basis as the other citrus fruits—thin skins, heaviness, uniform shapes. Keep them chilled in the refrigerator.

Most American *grapes* are grown west of the Rockies. Buy only plump fruit that does not drop from the stem when gently shaken. Grapes make wonderful table decorations, also, either alone or in combination with other fruits. Varieties most often found in markets include the seedless green Thompson grapes, the red Tokays, and the blue Concords for jellies. Refrigerate them immediately; grapes will not keep for long periods of time.

Pineapple should be naturally ripened for good flavor, although it will ripen at home. Keep it at room temperature, out of sunlight, until its top leafy spikes separate and will pull out easily. A strong, full pineapple aroma is another indication of ripeness. Since a pineapple ripens from the bottom up, avoid those that are soft around the bottom; the fruit is beginning to spoil.

The *peach* is a highly delicate fruit and must be carefully handled. Although a peach must be picked before it has reached full ripeness, do not buy a green peach; it will simply shrivel away. Buy only those with a rich, peach fragrance that are not withered or spotted. The Elberta is the most popular variety.

Plums are grown mainly in the western United States and there are many varieties. The type known as Damson is used strictly for cooking and canning. Plums vary tremendously in both size and color, ranging from green to rich, dark purple and from the size of a marble to that of an egg. Choose only those that yield slightly to a gentle touch; do not buy overripe plums. Keep them in a dark, airy place or in the refrigerator as you do apples.

Pears are one of the few fruits that are best picked green. Several of the many varieties of pears are available during each season of the year. Although Bartletts are considered the best eating pears, the harder-fleshed Seckels, Boscs, Comices, and Anjous are also offered in our markets. Other varieties range in color from green to russet. Buy them firm and allow them to ripen at room temperature at home.

APPLE-MINT MOLD

½ cup boiling water
1 package (3 ounces) lime-flavored gelatin
¼ cup lime juice
1 cup canned applesauce

⅛ teaspoon peppermint extract
½ cup coarsely chopped walnuts

Salad greens

1. Pour boiling water over gelatin in medium-size bowl, stirring to dissolve gelatin. Add lime juice. Refrigerate until consistency of unbeaten egg white—about 30 minutes.

2. Fold in applesauce, peppermint extract, and walnuts, combining well.

3. Turn into a 2-cup mold.

4. Refrigerate about 2 hours, or until firm.

5. To unmold: Run a small spatula around edge of mold. Invert over platter; shake gently to release. If necessary, place a hot, wet dishcloth over bottom of mold; shake again to release. Garnish with salad greens. Serve with leg of lamb, if desired.

Makes 6 servings.

STUFFED APRICOTS

¾ cup creamed cottage cheese   8 to 10 whole unpeeled
1 tablespoon snipped chives   apricots

1. In small bowl, combine cottage cheese and chives.

2. Remove pits from apricots; fill each with slightly rounded tablespoonful of cheese mixture.

3. Refrigerate, covered, until well chilled—about 1 hour.

Makes 8 to 10.

AVOCADO CREAM IN FROSTED ORANGE SHELLS

6 large navel oranges   1 avocado (about ¾ pound)
1 egg white, slightly beaten
1 cup sugar   Crushed ice
1 teaspoon unflavored gelatin   Mint sprigs

1. Cut a 1-inch-thick slice from top of each orange. Also cut just enough from bottom of each so orange will stand upright.

2. Holding oranges over bowl to collect juice, carefully scoop orange pulp out of shells. Drain juice from pulp into measuring cup; set aside ½ cup juice. Cut orange pulp into bite-size pieces; measure 2 cups. Refrigerate.

3. Brush rim and outside of orange shells with egg white. Place ½ cup sugar on waxed paper, and roll shells in it, to coat well. Place on wire rack; refrigerate.

4. Sprinkle gelatin over reserved orange juice; let stand 5 minutes, to soften. Set over hot water; stir until dissolved.

5. Halve avocado; remove pit and peel. Place avocado in electric-blender container with remaining sugar and the gelatin mixture. Blend avocado mixture at high speed until smooth.

6. Refrigerate, covered, just until set—about 2 hours.

7. To serve: Place frosted orange shells in crushed ice in dessert dishes. Divide orange pieces into shells, reserving 6 for garnish. Beat avocado cream with wooden spoon until smooth. Mound in orange shells. Decorate with reserved orange pieces and mint sprigs.

Makes 6 servings.

BAKED BANANAS

6 to 8 slightly underripe bananas	½ cup light-brown sugar, firmly
½ cup diced orange	packed
2 tablespoons orange juice	Dash cinnamon
2 tablespoons lemon juice	Dash nutmeg

1. Preheat the oven to 325°F.

2. Peel bananas. Arrange in shallow baking dish.

3. In small bowl, combine remaining ingredients. Spoon over bananas.

4. Bake, basting twice with pan juices, 30 minutes, or until bananas are golden and tender. Serve hot.

Makes 6 to 8 servings.

HARVEST FRUIT BOWL

2 large oranges	½ cup marsala
2 pink grapefruit	½ cup apricot nectar
1 red apple	¼ cup sugar
1 ripe pear	½ cup pitted dates
½ pound Tokay grapes	

1. Peel oranges and grapefruit, removing white membrane. With sharp knife, cut sections into a large bowl, holding fruit over bowl to catch juice.

2. Wash, quarter, and core apple and pear. Cut into ½-inch pieces. Add to orange and grapefruit sections.

3. Halve grapes; remove seeds. Add to fruits in bowl, together with marsala, apricot nectar, and sugar. Toss to mix well. Refrigerate, covered, overnight, or until well chilled.

4. An hour before serving, cut dates in half. Add to fruit mixture. Serve with poundcake, if desired.

Makes 10 to 12 servings.

SHERRIED FRUIT CUP

2 cups cantaloupe or Persian-melon balls

2 cups fresh strawberries, cut in half

2 cups fresh blueberries

¼ cup sugar

⅓ cup sherry or orange juice

2 tablespoons brandy or cognac (optional)

8 fresh mint sprigs

1. Combine melon balls, strawberries, blueberries, sugar, sherry, and brandy in large bowl.

2. Refrigerate, covered, until well chilled—several hours or overnight—stirring once.

3. Spoon into 8 dessert dishes. Garnish with mint sprigs.

Makes 8 servings.

FRESH-FRUIT EXTRAVAGANZA

1 large pineapple
1 honeydew melon
1 cantaloupe
1 lime
1 lemon

Large bunches green grapes (2 to 3 pounds)
3 or 4 large peaches
3 or 4 large pears

1. Cut pineapple: Using sharp knife, cut a thick slice from top, removing frond; set frond aside.

2. Remove rind from pineapple, cutting from top to bottom.

3. With tip of sharp paring knife, cut V-shape wedges to remove eyes, cutting on the diagonal. Cut pineapple crosswise into ½-inch-thick slices. Put back in place, to re-form pineapple. Place frond on top.

4. Cut melons into wedges; peel.

5. Cut lime into slices, lemon into 8 wedges, leaving them attached at bottom, to resemble a flower.

6. Arrange all fruit attractively on large platter. Cut 1 or 2 pears in half, if desired, and brush cut surfaces with lemon juice.

7. Refrigerate until ready to use. Place on buffet table as a centerpiece. Let guests serve themselves with fruit.

Makes 12 servings.

MOLDED FRUIT-AND-GINGER SALAD

1 can (13½ ounces) pineapple chunks

2⅓ cups boiling water

1 package (6 ounces) orange-pineapple-flavored gelatin

1 package (1 pound) frozen cantaloupe and honeydew-melon balls, thawed and drained

¼ cup finely chopped crystallized ginger

Parsley sprigs

1. Drain pineapple chunks, reserving ⅔ cup syrup.

2. Pour the boiling water over gelatin in large bowl, stirring to dissolve gelatin. Add reserved pineapple syrup.

3. Refrigerate until the consistency of unbeaten egg white—about 1 hour.

4. Fold in fruit and ginger. Turn into a 4½-cup mold. Refrigerate until firm—2 to 3 hours.

5. To unmold: Run a small spatula around edge of mold. Invert over platter; shake gently to release. If necessary, place a hot, wet dishcloth over bottom of mold; shake again to release. Garnish with parsley.

Makes 4 to 6 servings.

SUMMER-FRUIT SALAD WITH BLUE-CHEESE DRESSING

Blue-Cheese Dressing
½   cup mayonnaise or cooked
     salad dressing
¼   cup bottled herb dressing
½   cup crumbled blue cheese
2   tablespoons milk
2   tablespoons lemon juice

3   fresh pears
2   tablespoons lemon juice
3   navel oranges
1   pint box blueberries
1   pint box large strawberries,
     unhulled
4   cups honeydew-melon balls
Crisp iceberg lettuce

1. Make Blue-Cheese Dressing: In small bowl, combine mayonnaise, herb dressing, blue cheese, milk, and 2 tablespoons lemon juice. Beat until well combined.
2. Refrigerate dressing, covered.
3. Pare pears; halve; core. Dip pears in lemon juice. Peel oranges, removing any white membrane; cut each orange crosswise into 6 slices. Wash blueberries, strawberries; drain. Refrigerate fruit until ready to use.
4. To serve: Arrange lettuce leaves on 6 chilled salad plates. Place pear halves, cut side up, on lettuce; spoon blueberries evenly over pears.
5. Arrange 3 orange slices and ⅔ cup melon balls around pear on each plate. Garnish with strawberries.
6. Serve dressing over salad.
Makes 6 servings.

BROILED GRAPEFRUIT

1   grapefruit, halved
2   tablespoons honey

Cinnamon
Butter or margarine

1. Loosen sections of each grapefruit half with a sharp knife.
2. Spoon 1 tablespoon honey on each half; sprinkle tops with cinnamon; dot with butter.
3. Put under broiler 5 to 8 minutes, or until heated through.
Makes 2 servings.

GRILLED GRAPEFRUIT WITH KIRSCH

4 grapefruit, halved
1 cup sugar
1 cup kirsch

Mint sprigs (optional)
Maraschino cherries (optional)

1. Cut out centers and remove seeds from each grapefruit half. Cut around each section with grapefruit knife, to loosen.
2. Sprinkle each half with 2 tablespoons sugar, then with 2 tablespoons kirsch.
3. Broil, 4 inches from heat, about 5 minutes, or until bubbly and brown. Garnish with maraschino cherries and mint sprigs, if desired.
Makes 8 servings.

FRESH GRAPEFRUIT HALVES WITH ORANGE SECTIONS

2 grapefruit, chilled
4 teaspoons honey
2 oranges, sectioned, chilled,
   and drained

Mint leaves

1. Halve grapefruit. Cut out centers, and remove any seeds. With grapefruit knife, cut around each section, to loosen.
2. Drizzle each half with 1 teaspoon honey. Lift alternate sections of grapefruit, and place an orange section behind each.
3. Place remaining orange sections in center of halves. Garnish with mint.
Makes 4 servings.

FRESH-FRUIT MELON-GO-ROUND

1 large Spanish or honeydew
   melon
8 unpeeled nectarines or
   peaches

1½ pounds grapes
Fresh mint sprigs

1. Using sharp knife, cut ¼-inch slice from bottom of melon. Halve melon lengthwise; cut each half into 5 even wedges. Remove seeds.
2. Use a round serving platter, 9 inches in diameter and about ½ inch deep. Stand wedges, cut end down, to resemble a whole melon, holding wedges together at top, while placing a nectarine at base of alternate slices, to hold melon in place. Gently pull out the slices not held by nectarines. Secure top of wedges with wooden picks.
3. Garnish with remaining nectarines, small bunches of grapes, and mint sprigs.
Makes 8 servings.

HONEYDEW MELON CARIOCA

1 large ripe honeydew melon   ⅓ cup light rum
1 tablespoon light corn syrup

1. Cut a slice crosswise from stem end of melon (about 3 inches); set aside. Scoop out seeds and pulp.
2. Add corn syrup to rum in a measuring cup; mix well. Pour into melon.
3. Replace slice, and hold in place with long wooden picks or skewers. Roll melon over gently, so rum-and-syrup mixture will coat inside. Stand melon upright in a medium-size bowl. Refrigerate 8 hours or overnight.
4. To serve: Remove top slice; pour liquid from melon into small pitcher. Cut melon into 8 wedges. Pass pitcher of liquid.
Makes 8 servings.

HONEYDEW-MELON BALLS IN CRÈME DE MENTHE

4 cups honeydew-melon balls   3 tablespoons light corn syrup
2½ tablespoons white crème de
    menthe   6 fresh mint sprigs

1. In medium-size bowl, combine melon balls, crème de menthe, corn syrup.

2. Refrigerate, covered, until well chilled—about 2 hours.
3. To serve: Spoon into six dessert dishes. Garnish with mint.
Makes 6 servings.

HONEYDEW-AND-GREEN-GRAPE FANTASY

1 large honeydew melon (about   Daisies with green leaves
   4 pounds)
Clusters of seedless green grapes
   (about 3 pounds)

1. Cut melon into 8 wedges, leaving them attached at bottom.
Remove seeds and pulp, and discard.
2. Carefully cut between melon rind and fruit to within 2 to 3 inches
of bottom of wedges. Stand melon in a shallow dish about 8 inches in
diameter.
3. Fill center of melon with grape clusters, mounding high.
4. Decorate with daisies, inserting stems between grape clusters.
5. Refrigerate until ready to use. Place on table as a centerpiece. Let
guests serve themselves with fruit.
Makes 8 servings.

CANTALOUPE BALLS À L'ORANGE

¼ cup slightly thawed frozen   1 tablespoon kirsch
   orange-juice concentrate,   4 cups cantaloupe balls
   undiluted
2 tablespoons light corn syrup   6 fresh mint sprigs

1. In medium-size bowl, combine orange-juice concentrate, corn
syrup, and kirsch; mix well.
2. Add melon balls; toss lightly to combine.
3. Refrigerate, covered, until well chilled—about 2 hours.
4. To serve: Spoon into six dessert dishes. Garnish with mint.
Makes 6 servings.

MELON-BALL COUPE

1   tablespoon lime juice
1   tablespoon honey
⅛   teaspoon ground ginger
1   cup cantaloupe balls

1   cup honeydew-melon balls

Lime wedges

1. Combine lime juice, honey, and ginger.
2. Add melon balls; toss to coat well. Refrigerate at least 1 hour.
3. Garnish with lime wedges, and serve.
Makes 2 cups.

MELON BALLS MELBA

Sauce
1   cup fresh raspberries
1   tablespoon snipped fresh
     mint
2   tablespoons sugar
3   tablespoons golden rum
4   cups watermelon or
     honeydew-melon balls

1   navel orange, peeled and
     sliced

Fresh mint sprigs

1. Make Sauce: Press raspberries through sieve to make a purée.
2. Combine raspberry purée with snipped mint, sugar, and rum, mixing well.
3. In large bowl, gently mix melon balls with the raspberry sauce.
4. Refrigerate, covered, for several hours.
5. To serve: Turn melon-ball mixture into chilled cut-glass serving bowl. Cut orange slices in half; place around edge of bowl. Garnish with mint sprigs.
Makes 6 servings.

MELON-BASKET CENTERPIECE

1 medium-size watermelon (about 12 pounds)	Ivy
2 cups honeydew-melon balls	Lemon wedges (optional)
2 cups cantaloupe balls	

1. Cut slice from one end of watermelon, so it will stand upright. Stand watermelon on cut end.

2. Mark center top of melon. Then measure ¾ inch on each side, to make a 1½-inch-wide handle. Cut out melon wedge on each side of handle. Then carefully cut fruit away from rind at top, to form handle.

3. Now make a rickrack edge. With a small, sharp knife, carve a second rickrack line for decoration. Cut balls from melon; then scoop out remaining fruit, to make basket.

4. Fill basket with watermelon, honeydew, and cantaloupe balls; mound high. Wrap handle with ivy.

5. Refrigerate until ready to use. Place on table as a centerpiece. Let guests serve themselves with melon balls. Serve with lemon wedges, if desired.

Makes 8 servings.

CINNAMON ORANGES

3 oranges	¼ teaspoon cinnamon
¼ cup sugar	

1. Peel oranges; slice crosswise, ¼ inch thick. Arrange in shallow dish.

2. Combine sugar and cinnamon. Toss oranges with sugar mixture, to coat well. Refrigerate until well chilled—at least 1 hour.

Makes 6 servings.

GLAZED ORANGE SLICES

3 medium oranges	½ cup brown sugar, firmly
¼ cup butter or margarine	packed
	2 tablespoons light corn syrup

1. Trim and discard ends from oranges.
2. Cut unpeeled oranges crosswise into slices, about ½ inch thick.
3. In large skillet, combine butter, brown sugar, and corn syrup; cook over medium heat, stirring, until sugar is melted and mixture boils.
4. Layer orange slices in skillet; cook, uncovered, 5 minutes. Turn slices, and cook 5 minutes longer, or just until orange slices are shiny and glazed.

Makes 6 servings.

ORANGES ORIENTALE

8 large navel or Temple oranges	¼ cup lemon juice
1½ cups sugar	¼ cup cointreau
1½ cups light corn syrup	
Red food coloring	**Candied violets (optional)**

1. With sharp paring knife, remove peel from 4 oranges in 1½-inch-long strips. Remove any white membrane from strips. Cut each lengthwise into ⅛-inch-wide pieces. (Or, if desired, remove peel with a coarse grater.) Makes about 1 cup.
2. Peel remaining oranges; discard peel. Remove any white membrane from all oranges. Place oranges, whole or cut in half, in large bowl; set aside.
3. In small saucepan, combine prepared peel with 2 cups cold water. Bring to boil, covered. Remove from heat; drain. Reserve peel.
4. In large saucepan, combine sugar and corn syrup with a few drops red food coloring and 1½ cups water; bring to boil over high heat, stirring until sugar is dissolved. Cook, uncovered and over medium heat, 10 minutes. Add reserved peel.

5. Continue cooking 30 minutes longer, or until syrup is slightly thickened. Remove from heat; stir in lemon juice and cointreau.

6. Pour hot syrup over oranges in bowl. Refrigerate, covered, at least 8 hours; turn oranges occasionally.

7. Serve chilled oranges topped with some of the syrup and candied peel. Decorate, if desired, with candied violets. Serve with dessert forks and fruit knives.

Makes 8 servings.

ORANGE-PEACH COMPOTE

4 large peaches, peeled and quartered	½ cup orange juice
2 large oranges, peeled and sectioned	¼ cup sugar
	1 tablespoon golden rum

1. In serving bowl, combine peach quarters and orange sections.

2. Add orange juice. Sprinkle fruit with sugar and rum; mix gently, to coat fruit.

3. Refrigerate, covered, 2 hours, or until well chilled.

4. Mix gently just before serving.

Makes 6 servings.

PEACH-CURRANT SALAD MOLD

1 can (1 pound, 13 ounces) cling-peach halves	2 tablespoons orange marmalade
1 cup boiling water	2 tablespoons toasted slivered almonds
1 package (3 ounces) peach-flavored gelatin	
2 tablespoons currant jelly	Salad greens

1. Drain peaches, reserving 1 cup syrup.

2. Pour boiling water over gelatin, stirring to dissolve gelatin. Add reserved syrup from peaches.

3. Pour 3 tablespoons gelatin mixture into each of 6 (6-ounce) custard cups. Refrigerate until firm—about 15 minutes.

4. Refrigerate remaining gelatin mixture until consistency of unbeaten egg white—about 1 hour.

5. In small bowl, combine currant jelly, marmalade, and almonds. Place 1 tablespoon mixture on top of set gelatin in each custard cup.

6. Invert a peach half over jelly mixture in each custard cup.

7. Pour rest of gelatin mixture over peaches. Refrigerate until firm—about 2 hours, or overnight.

8. To unmold: Run a small spatula around edge of custard cup. Invert over platter; shake gently to release. If necessary, place a hot, wet dishcloth over bottom of cup; shake again to release.

9. Garnish with salad greens. Serve with ham or turkey, if desired. Makes 6 servings.

HOT CURRIED PEACHES

¼ cup light-brown sugar, firmly packed
½ teaspoon curry powder
1 can (1 pound, 14 ounces) cling-peach halves, drained

3 tablespoons butter or margarine

1. Preheat oven to 375°F. Combine brown sugar and curry powder.

2. Place peach halves, cut side up, in 9-inch pie plate. Dot with the butter, and sprinkle with the brown-sugar mixture.

3. Bake 10 minutes, or until sugar darkens slightly. Serve with ham or bacon and eggs.

Makes 7 or 8 servings.

PEACHES IN PORT

2 cans (1-pound, 14-ounce size) sliced cling peaches

Dash cardamom or nutmeg
¾ cup port

1. Drain peaches, reserving 3 tablespoons syrup. Place peaches in shallow dish.

2. Combine the reserved syrup, cardamom, and wine; pour over the peaches.

3. Refrigerate, covered, for 4 to 6 hours.

4. To serve, turn peaches and liquid into serving bowl.
Makes 6 servings.

FRESH PEARS IN MAPLE SYRUP

½ cup maple syrup
¼ cup orange juice
2 tablespoons lemon juice

4 large pears, peeled, cored, and quartered
1 tablespoon coarsely grated orange peel

1. Combine maple syrup and orange and lemon juices in medium-size skillet. Add pears; mix gently, to coat fruit.

2. Cover; bring to a boil. Reduce heat, and simmer gently 5 minutes. Remove from heat. Turn into serving bowl. Sprinkle with grated orange peel.

3. Refrigerate, covered, 2 hours, or until well chilled.
Makes 4 to 6 servings.

PINEAPPLE AU NATUREL

4 cups fresh pineapple chunks
1 tablespoon granulated sugar
1 cup dairy sour cream

3 tablespoons light-brown sugar
⅛ teaspoon nutmeg

1. In medium-size bowl, sprinkle pineapple chunks with granulated sugar. Refrigerate, covered, 1 hour, or until well chilled.

2. Just before serving: In small bowl, with electric mixer, beat sour cream, brown sugar, and nutmeg until smooth.

3. To serve: Spoon pineapple chunks into 8 sherbet dishes. Top with sour-cream mixture. Sprinkle with more brown sugar, if desired.
Makes 8 servings.

FRESH PINEAPPLE DE MENTHE

1 large ripe pineapple (3½ to 4 pounds)
⅓ cup green crème de menthe
1 egg white

Sugar
Chocolate leaves or cookies (optional)

1. With sharp knife, cut off frond of pineapple, and reserve. Cut 1-inch slice from bottom; discard. Remove rind by cutting down the pineapple in wide slices. Remove eyes by cutting V-shape wedges full length of pineapple, following diagonal pattern of eyes; lift out wedges, and discard.

2. Cut pineapple crosswise into 6 slices; remove core, and discard. Keeping slices in order for reassembling easily later, arrange in loaf pan. Drizzle crème de menthe over slices to coat evenly. Refrigerate, covered, several hours; turn occasionally.

3. Meanwhile, decorate reserved frond: Slightly beat egg white with 1 tablespoon water; brush over frond. Sprinkle with sugar, shaking off excess. Let dry at room temperature several hours.

4. To serve: Stack chilled pineapple slices on serving plate to resemble whole pineapple. Top with decorated frond. If desired, set frond on paper doily before placing on slices. Surround pineapple with chocolate leaves or other party cookies, if desired.

Makes 6 servings.

POACHED PLUMS CARDAMOM

¾ cup sugar
1 tablespoon lemon juice
¼ teaspoon ground cardamom

3 cups halved, pitted, unpeeled purple or red plums

Dairy sour cream

1. In medium-size saucepan, combine sugar with 1 cup water. Over high heat, bring to boil, stirring to dissolve sugar. Boil, uncovered, 10 minutes.

2. Add lemon juice, cardamom, and plums; reduce heat; simmer, covered, about 4 minutes.

3. Let plums cool in syrup; then refrigerate until they are very well chilled.

4. To serve: Spoon plums and syrup into serving dishes. Top each with a spoonful of sour cream.

Makes 4 to 6 servings.

BAKED FRESH RHUBARB

4 cups cut rhubarb, in 1-inch pieces (about 1¾ pounds)
1 cup sugar
1-inch cinnamon stick
4 whole cloves

1. Preheat oven to 400°F.
2. Place rhubarb in a 2-quart casserole. Sprinkle with sugar; add cinnamon and cloves.
3. Bake, covered, 20 minutes. Stir gently, to dissolve sugar. Baste fruit; bake 10 minutes, or until rhubarb is tender but not mushy.
4. Let stand, covered, on wire rack until cool.

Makes 4 to 6 servings.

RHUBARB-AND-PINEAPPLE COMPOTE

4 cups cut rhubarb, in 1-inch pieces (about 1¾ pounds)
1 cup sugar
1-inch cinnamon stick
4 whole cloves
1 package (12 ounces) frozen pineapple chunks

1. Preheat oven to 400°F.
2. Place rhubarb in a 2-quart casserole. Sprinkle with sugar; add cinnamon and cloves.
3. Bake, covered, 20 minutes. Stir gently, to dissolve sugar. Baste fruit; bake 10 minutes, or until rhubarb is tender but not mushy. Stir in frozen pineapple.
4. Let stand, covered, on wire rack until cool. Serve chilled, if desired.

Makes 6 servings.

STRAWBERRIES ROMANOFF

2 pint boxes fresh strawberries
1 cup confectioners' sugar
1 cup heavy cream

1 teaspoon almond extract
2 tablespoons cointreau or orange juice

1. Gently wash strawberries in cold water; drain; hull.
2. In medium-size bowl, sprinkle sugar over berries; toss gently.
3. Refrigerate 1 hour, stirring occasionally.
4. In chilled bowl, with rotary beater, whip cream until stiff. Add almond extract and cointreau.
5. Fold into strawberries. Serve at once.
Makes 8 servings.

WINTER-SALAD MOLD

2 envelopes unflavored gelatin
1 can (6 ounces) frozen grapefruit-juice concentrate, undiluted
3 ice cubes

1 can (1 pound) grapefruit sections, undrained
½ cup diced celery
½ cup diced, unpared red apple

Salad greens

1. Sprinkle gelatin over ¾ cup cold water in medium-size saucepan; let stand 5 minutes to soften. Over low heat, stir until gelatin is dissolved.
2. Remove from heat. Add grapefruit juice and ice cubes; stir until ice is dissolved.
3. Add grapefruit, celery, and apple. Turn into a 1-quart mold. Refrigerate until firm—2 to 3 hours.
4. To unmold: Run a small spatula around edge of mold. Invert over platter; shake gently to release. If necessary, place a hot, wet dishcloth over bottom of mold; shake again to release. Garnish with salad greens.
Makes 6 servings.

3

EGGS

Eggs are healthful and delicious, the ideal way to begin the day. There has been a good deal of concern in the last few years about high cholesterol counts, yet nutritionists claim that the type of fat used to cook the egg, not the egg itself, is probably the source of the high cholesterol content. Vegetable oil should be used in cooking since it does not raise the cholesterol level. Eggs are one of our best sources of protein, and they also furnish a generous supply of vitamins A and B2.

In order to produce a perfect egg dish, you must begin by using the very freshest eggs, preferably less than a week old. There is actually no difference between white and brown eggs, although various cooks do have their preferences.

Eggs are graded AA, A, B, or C. In a Grade AA egg, the white will be more jellylike and the yolk rounder, firmer, and more centered than that of the Grade B or C egg. Grade B and C eggs are quite acceptable, however, for preparing any dish that does not require a perfect fried or poached egg.

The basic rule in cooking eggs is to use very low heat, since protein toughens when subjected to high heats.

To *boil* eggs, allow them to reach room temperature, and then slip them carefully into a deep pan containing boiling water. Cover and bring water back to boiling point. Immediately remove pan from heat and allow to stand no longer than ten minutes for soft-boiled, and no longer than a half hour for hard-boiled. (If you haven't time to allow eggs to warm to room temperature, place them in a pan of cold water and bring it to a boil.) Serve soft-boiled eggs immediately; allow hard-boiled eggs to stand twenty minutes. For a different taste, chop and cream boiled eggs, seasoned to your taste, and serve on toast or toasted scones.

The common method of *frying* eggs is to heat one or two tablespoons of butter or margarine in a skillet until the fat sizzles and then carefully break the desired number of eggs into it. Remove from the heat immediately and baste with hot fat for several minutes. Or, to eliminate the butter and to ensure preservation of the vitamins, lightly brush a moderately hot skillet with oil, break the eggs into it, and add two tablespoons milk or water. Cover and cook over lowest possible heat until white is firm—about fifteen minutes. To eliminate the use of fat entirely, use a Teflon-lined skillet to "fry" your eggs. When cooking with an electric skillet, set the temperature to about 275°F. and proceed as above.

To *bake* eggs, break them into shallow baking dishes that have been oiled and place them in a 325°F. oven for fifteen minutes, or until set. For a pleasant variation, sprinkle grated cheese over the eggs three or four minutes before they are done and then serve with bacon and sautéed eggplant or tomato slices.

Scrambled eggs may be premixed in stainless steel, glass, or enameled bowls. Do not use aluminum or silver since the sulfur in eggs will discolor them. Add a tablespoon of water or milk and salt and pepper and beat with a stainless steel fork or wire whip until well mixed. Brush the skillet with oil and heat it until it sizzles. Pour in the egg mixture and cook over extremely low heat until they are set, stirring occasionally to produce soft, creamy eggs. To preserve vitamins, keep the skillet covered as much as possible.

Poached eggs must be prepared with only the freshest of ingredients, since it is essential that the white congeal properly. Bring from one-and-one-half to two inches of water (broth or milk may also be used) to a boil. Add salt to taste. Reduce heat until water is barely simmering. Break each egg into a saucer and slip the egg into the water. Cover and allow the water to simmer until whites are firm, about three to five minutes. Remove with a slotted utensil and drain. Cover with a cream or curry sauce or a seafood newburg for a tantalizing brunch dish.

In order to ensure successful *omelets* and *soufflés,* use eggs that have been allowed to reach room temperature and cook them over a very low heat. Special cooking utensils are also helpful. An omelet pan—which has rounded sides—is invaluable for omelet-making and it should be reserved only for that purpose. The surface should be wiped, not washed, with a paper towel after each use. If you have no omelet pan, you can "season" any skillet by scouring it thoroughly, filling it with an inch or so of oil, and setting it over a low fire for fifteen minutes. After discarding the oil, wipe the skillet dry with paper towels.

Since a soufflé requires stiffly beaten egg whites, a copper bowl will be an aid. Copper reacts chemically with egg whites, producing a denser consistency in the whites. If you do not own a copper bowl, add a pinch of cream of tartar for each egg white. In any case, it is essential that both the mixing bowl and the beaters be completely free of fat, since fat breaks down the structure of the egg-white foam, causing it to lose height. When adding the beaten whites to the remaining mixture, fold them in very gently, being careful not to break them down. A rubber scraper is a good implement to use for this. When the mixture is ready for baking, pour it into an oiled soufflé dish or any nonaluminum ovenproof utensil that has straight sides—the sides must be straight so that the soufflé can cling to them while it is rising. Dusting the bottom of the dish with bread crumbs, Parmesan cheese, or superfine sugar will aid in producing a perfect result. When the soufflé has finished baking, serve it immediately. There are endless variations of omelets and soufflés, which will result in main-course dishes, side dishes, or desserts. Choose from among the recipes that follow or make your own creations by adding leftovers of meat, fish, and vegetables. Cheese, of course, is a delicious addition, and finely diced beef, pork, veal, or tongue, combined with chopped onion and seasonings of your choice, will make a good main dish. Bacon, ham, chicken livers, and chopped shrimp or other seafood also make fine additions. For vegetable omelets or soufflés, try using peas, mushrooms, pimiento, and bean sprouts. Garnish with parsley and sautéed tomatoes. Chopped chicken liver combined with chopped onion will make an omelet fit for the most discriminating guest.

EGG CROQUETTES WITH BÉCHAMEL SAUCE

Croquettes

3 tablespoons butter or
   margarine
¼ cup unsifted all-purpose flour
1 cup milk
8 hard-cooked eggs, coarsely
   chopped
½ teaspoon salt
½ teaspoon paprika

¼ teaspoon pepper
1 teaspoon finely chopped
   onion
1 tablespoon chopped parsley
Dash nutmeg
½ cup packaged dry bread
   crumbs

Béchamel Sauce

3 tablespoons butter or
   margarine
¼ cup unsifted all-purpose flour
1 cup canned chicken broth,
   undiluted
¼ teaspoon salt
⅛ teaspoon pepper
⅛ teaspoon paprika
½ cup light cream

Salad oil or shortening for
   deep-frying
1 cup unsifted all-purpose flour
2 eggs
1½ cups packaged dry bread
   crumbs

1. Make Croquettes: Melt butter in medium-size saucepan. Remove from heat. Add flour, stirring until smooth.

2. Gradually stir in milk; bring to boil, stirring constantly. Remove from heat.

3. Add chopped eggs and rest of croquette ingredients; mix gently.

4. Refrigerate about 1 hour, or until ready to use.

5. Make Sauce: Melt 1 tablespoon butter in small saucepan. Remove from heat.

6. Stir in flour until smooth. Gradually stir in chicken broth. Add salt, pepper, and paprika; bring to boil, stirring.

7. Reduce heat; keep warm. Just before serving, stir in cream and rest of butter, cut into small bits.

8. Meanwhile, in deep skillet or deep-fat fryer, slowly heat salad oil (at least 2 inches deep) to 385°F. on deep-frying thermometer.

9. Shape croquette mixture into 18 (2-inch) ovals.

10. Roll lightly in flour, then roll in eggs, which have been beaten with ¼ cup water. Roll in crumbs to coat completely.

11. Deep-fry croquettes, a few at a time, 3 to 4 minutes, or until golden-brown. Drain thoroughly on paper towels. Serve hot with Béchamel Sauce.

Makes 6 servings.

EGGS RANCHO

Sauce

3 bacon slices, diced
1 teaspoon cornstarch
¼ cup finely chopped onion
1 cup finely chopped green pepper
⅔ cup chili sauce
⅓ cup dark corn syrup
2 tablespoons lemon juice
1½ teaspoons Worcestershire sauce

2 tablespoons butter or margarine
6 eggs
3 (3½-ounce) minute steaks
¼ cup grated sharp Cheddar cheese

1. Make Sauce: Over low heat, sauté bacon until crisp. Drain excess fat.

2. Combine cornstarch with 3 tablespoons water. Add to bacon along with onion, green pepper, chili sauce, corn syrup, lemon juice, and Worcestershire.

3. Bring to boil; reduce heat, and simmer 10 minutes, stirring occasionally.

4. Meanwhile, slowly heat butter in large skillet. Break eggs directly into pan. Over low heat, sauté eggs gently until of desired doneness—3 or 4 minutes.

5. Cook steaks to taste.

6. To serve: Top each steak with some sauce, then with an egg. Sprinkle each egg with cheese.

Makes 6 servings.

BAKED EGGS GRUYÈRE

1 package (6 ounces) individual Gruyère-cheese wedges	6 eggs
	½ cup heavy cream
10 crisp-cooked bacon slices	⅛ teaspoon pepper

1. Preheat oven to 350°F. Generously butter a 10- by 6- by 2-inch baking dish.
2. Cut each of 5 cheese wedges lengthwise into fourths. Cover bottom of prepared dish with cheese slices.
3. Crumble bacon over cheese in dish. Carefully break eggs over cheese and bacon.
4. Spoon cream over eggs; sprinkle with pepper.
5. Grate remaining cheese wedge; sprinkle over eggs.
6. Bake, uncovered, 20 minutes, or just until eggs are set.
Makes 6 servings.

CRUNCHY BAKED EGGS

6 bacon slices, diced	Pepper
2 cups cornflakes, crushed	4 teaspoons grated Parmesan cheese
8 eggs	
Salt	

1. Preheat oven to 375°F. Grease 4 (10-ounce) custard cups.
2. In medium-size skillet, sauté bacon until crisp. Remove from skillet; drain on paper towels.
3. Pour off bacon drippings; return 2 tablespoons to skillet.
4. Add cornflakes to skillet; toss to coat with drippings.
5. Sprinkle about 1 tablespoon bacon in bottom of each prepared custard cup.
6. With back of spoon, press cornflake mixture against sides of cups, around bacon, to form a nest. Use about ¼ cup for each nest.
7. Gently slip eggs (2 at a time) into nests. Sprinkle with salt and pepper to taste. Bake 10 minutes.
8. Sprinkle with cheese; bake 5 to 7 minutes longer, or until of desired doneness.
Makes 4 servings.

SHIRRED EGGS À LA SUISSE

Butter or margarine
6 tablespoons fresh bread crumbs
12 slices natural Swiss cheese (½ pound)
6 large tomato slices
Dried thyme leaves
¾ cup heavy cream
6 eggs
¼ teaspoon salt
⅛ teaspoon pepper
⅛ teaspoon paprika
2 tablespoons grated Parmesan cheese
6 buttered toast slices, crusts removed

1. Preheat oven to 425°F. Butter bottoms and sides of 6 (5-inch) ramekins.

2. Sprinkle 1 tablespoon bread crumbs in bottom of each.

3. Cover with 2 slices Swiss cheese, overlapping to cover bottom and sides of ramekin.

4. Top with a slice of tomato, sprinkled with a dash of thyme.

5. To each, add 1 tablespoon cream. Break egg on top. Cover each with 1 more tablespoon cream.

6. Sprinkle each with a little salt, pepper, paprika, and 1 teaspoon Parmesan cheese.

7. Bake, uncovered, 20 minutes, or just until eggs are set.

8. Cut toast into triangular quarters; arrange 4 triangles around edge of each ramekin.

Makes 6 servings.

CREAMY SCRAMBLED EGGS

7 eggs
¼ cup milk
½ teaspoon salt
Dash pepper
2 tablespoons butter or margarine
½ bar (6-ounce size) clam-lobster cream cheese, or 1 package (3 ounces) chive cream cheese, cut in ½-inch cubes

Fresh dill or parsley

1. In medium-size bowl, combine eggs, milk, salt, and pepper; with rotary beater, beat just until combined.

2. Heat butter in a large skillet. Pour in egg mixture; cook over low heat. As eggs start to set on bottom, gently lift cooked portion, with spatula, to form flakes, letting uncooked portion flow to bottom of pan.

3. Add cheese cubes; cook until eggs are moist and shiny but no longer runny.

4. Spoon onto heated serving plates. Sprinkle with snipped fresh dill or parsley.

Makes 4 or 5 servings.

DOUBLE-BOILER SCRAMBLED EGGS

8 eggs	¾ teaspoon salt
½ cup milk	⅛ teaspoon pepper

1. In top of double boiler, combine eggs, milk, salt, and pepper. With rotary beater, beat until well blended.

2. Cook over gently boiling water, stirring occasionally, 10 to 15 minutes, or until eggs are of desired doneness.

Makes 4 servings.

MEXICAN-STYLE SCRAMBLED EGGS

Sauce

1 tablespoon butter or margarine	½ cup finely chopped green pepper
1 small white onion, sliced	¼ cup finely chopped onion
1 tablespoon flour	1 clove garlic, crushed
1 can (1 pound) stewed tomatoes	6 eggs
	2 tablespoons milk
3 tablespoons butter or margarine	½ teaspoon salt
	⅛ teaspoon pepper

1. Make Sauce: Melt 1 tablespoon butter in small saucepan. Add sliced onion; sauté until soft. Remove from heat. Stir in flour until smooth. Gradually stir in tomatoes; bring to a boil, stirring. Reduce heat, and simmer 3 minutes. Keep warm.

2. In 3 tablespoons hot butter in skillet, sauté green pepper, chopped onion, and the garlic until tender—about 5 minutes.

3. In medium-size bowl, beat eggs with milk, salt, and pepper until well combined. Add to sautéed vegetables.

4. Cook over low heat. As eggs start to set, lift with spatula to let uncooked portion run underneath.

5. Place on warm serving platter, and surround with tomato sauce.

Makes 3 or 4 servings.

MUSHROOM SCRAMBLED EGGS

6 eggs	2 tablespoons butter or
1 tablespoon all-purpose flour	margarine
½ teaspoon salt	1 can (3 ounces) sliced
Dash pepper	mushrooms, drained
⅓ cup light cream	2 green onions, sliced
1 tablespoon dry sherry	
	Toast slices (optional)

1. In large bowl, with rotary beater, beat eggs until frothy. Sprinkle with flour, salt, and pepper; beat until smooth. Beat in cream and sherry.

2. Melt butter in a 9-inch skillet, over medium heat.

3. Pour egg mixture into skillet; cook slowly. As eggs start to set at bottom, gently lift cooked portion with spatula to form flakes, letting uncooked portion flow to bottom of skillet. Add mushrooms.

4. When eggs are cooked but still shiny and moist, remove from heat.

5. Turn into serving dish. Sprinkle with onions. Serve with crisp toast slices, if desired.

Makes 3 servings.

ROQUEFORT-CHEESE SCRAMBLED EGGS

8 eggs	1 bar (6 ounces) blue-cheese spread
½ cup milk	
½ teaspoon salt	
⅛ teaspoon pepper	Chopped parsley and parsley sprigs
1½ tablespoons butter or margarine	

1. In medium-size bowl, with electric mixer or rotary beater, beat eggs, milk, salt, and pepper until well blended.

2. In large skillet, heat butter over low heat. Add egg mixture; cook until eggs begin to set on bottom.

3. Stir gently, and continue cooking until eggs form creamy curds.

4. Meanwhile, cut cheese into about ½-inch cubes. Stir into eggs; continue cooking until eggs are almost set but still soft and cheese is slightly melted.

5. Garnish with chopped parsley and parsley sprigs. Makes 4 servings.

SHRIMP-AND-CRAB-MEAT SCRAMBLED EGGS

1 package (7 ounces) frozen shrimp	1 tablespoon chopped chives
1 can (7½ ounces) king-crab meat	12 eggs
	1 teaspoon seasoned salt
3 tablespoons dry sherry	1 teaspoon salt
6 tablespoons butter or margarine	⅛ teaspoon pepper
	Few drops Tabasco
2 tablespoons flour	
¾ cup milk	Chopped chives (optional)

1. Cook shrimp as package label directs; drain. Drain and flake crab meat.

2. In medium-size bowl, mix shrimp, crab meat, and sherry. Set aside.

3. Melt 2 tablespoons butter in medium-size saucepan. Remove from heat; stir in flour until smooth. Gradually stir in milk.

4. Bring to boil, stirring constantly. Reduce heat; simmer 1 minute. Stir in the chives and shrimp mixture. Set aside.

5. In large bowl, combine eggs, salts, pepper, and Tabasco; with rotary beater, beat until well combined.

6. In large skillet, heat remaining 4 tablespoons butter until bubbly. Pour in the egg mixture; cook over low heat. When bottom of egg begins to set, stir with a spatula until partially cooked.

7. Stir in seafood mixture; cook until eggs are done. Sprinkle with chopped chives, if desired.

Makes 6 servings.

EGGS BENEDICT

Hollandaise Sauce (see p. 60)	½ teaspoon salt
2 English muffins	4 eggs
Butter or margarine	
¼ pound fully cooked boneless ham, sliced	Watercress sprigs

1. Make Hollandaise Sauce.

2. Split muffins; butter cut sides. Arrange on cookie sheet; broil until golden. Keep warm.

3. Sauté ham until browned.

4. In medium-size skillet with tight-fitting cover, bring 1 inch water to simmering; add salt. Break 1 egg at a time into custard cup; slip egg into water. Simmer, covered, 3 to 5 minutes.

5. For each serving, overlap half of ham slices on 2 muffin halves side by side on cookie sheet. With slotted utensil, place 2 eggs on ham. Spoon on the Hollandaise. Then run under broiler until sauce is golden.

6. With broad spatula, remove to serving plates. Add the watercress. Serves 2.

HOLLANDAISE SAUCE

2 egg yolks
¼ cup butter or margarine, melted

1½ tablespoons lemon juice
¼ teaspoon salt
Dash cayenne

1. With a wire whisk or fork, beat egg yolks in top of double boiler.
2. Gradually pour in melted butter, beating constantly. Gradually add ¼ cup boiling water, beating constantly.
3. Cook, stirring, over hot, not boiling, water until mixture is thickened.
4. Remove double-boiler top from hot water. Gradually stir in lemon juice; add salt and cayenne. Set aside until ready to use for Eggs Benedict or Chicken Soufflé Hollandaise.

Makes ¾ cup.

POACHED EGGS NEWBURG

Shrimp-Newburg Sauce (see below)
6 eggs

6 buttered toast slices, crusts removed

1. Make Shrimp-Newburg Sauce. Keep warm in top of double boiler over hot water.
2. Poach eggs (see p. 50).
3. Place 1 egg on each slice of toast. Spoon on sauce.

Makes 6 servings.

SHRIMP-NEWBURG SAUCE

White Sauce

¼ cup butter or margarine
¼ cup unsifted all-purpose flour
1 teaspoon salt

⅛ teaspoon pepper
2 cups milk

2 slightly beaten egg yolks
2 tablespoons dry sherry
¼ teaspoon salt
Dash paprika

1 pound cooked deveined
   shrimp or 2 cans (5-ounce
   size) deveined shrimp,
   drained

1. Make White Sauce: In medium-size saucepan, slowly heat butter just until melted and golden, not browned, stirring all the while. Remove from heat.

2. Add flour, salt, and pepper; stir until mixture is smooth. Add milk, a small amount at a time, stirring after each addition. Return to heat.

3. Over medium heat, bring mixture to boiling point, stirring constantly. Reduce heat; simmer 1 minute.

4. Stir hot White Sauce, a small amount at a time, into egg yolks. Return to saucepan.

5. Add sherry, salt, paprika, and shrimp. Reheat, stirring.
Makes 3½ cups.

COTTAGE-CHEESE-AND-CHIVE OMELET

1 container (8 ounces)
   large-curd creamed cottage
   cheese
2 tablespoons snipped chives
1 teaspoon chopped parsley

6 eggs
½ teaspoon salt
⅛ teaspoon dry mustard
1 tablespoon butter or
   margarine

1. In small bowl, combine cottage cheese, chives, and parsley. Set aside.

2. In medium-size bowl, combine eggs, 1 tablespoon water, the salt, and mustard; beat with wire whisk until mixed but not foamy.

3. Meanwhile, slowly heat a 10-inch heavy skillet or omelet pan until a little cold water sizzles and rolls off in drops. Add butter; heat until it sizzles—do not brown.

4. Quickly turn egg mixture, all at once, into skillet; cook over medium heat. As mixture sets, run spatula around edge, to loosen; tilt pan, to let uncooked portion run underneath. Continue loosening and tilting until omelet is almost dry on top and golden brown underneath.

5. Spoon cottage-cheese mixture over half of omelet; fold over other half. Turn out onto serving plate.

Makes 4 servings.

FRENCH OMELET WITH CHICKEN LIVERS

4 slices bacon	½ teaspoon salt
½ pound chicken livers	½ teaspoon Worcestershire
½ cup chopped onion	sauce
½ cup coarsely chopped green pepper	

Omelet

6 eggs	2 tablespoons butter or
½ teaspoon salt	margarine

1. In skillet, fry bacon until crisp. Drain on paper towels; crumble.

2. Add chicken livers to bacon drippings in skillet; sauté 3 to 4 minutes. Remove with slotted utensil to board; chop coarsely.

3. Add onion and green pepper to skillet; sauté until tender—about 5 minutes. Add chicken liver, bacon, salt, Worcestershire, and ¼ cup water; heat gently. Cover, and keep warm.

4. Make Omelet: In medium-size bowl, with rotary beater, beat eggs with 3 tablespoons water and the salt until well blended but not frothy.

5. Slowly heat a 10-inch heavy skillet. Add butter, and heat until it sizzles briskly.

6. Turn egg mixture into skillet; cook over medium heat. As egg sets, run spatula around edge to loosen, and tilt pan to let uncooked portion run underneath. Continue loosening and tilting until omelet is almost dry on top and golden brown underneath.

7. Place chicken-liver mixture in center. Fold omelet in half, and slide onto heated serving plate.

Makes 6 servings.

OMELET FINES HERBES

3 eggs
¼ teaspoon salt
2 tablespoons finely snipped fresh parsley
1 teaspoon finely snipped fresh tarragon leaves
1 teaspoon finely snipped fresh marjoram leaves

½ teaspoon finely snipped fresh thyme leaves
1 teaspoon finely chopped shallots
1 tablespoon butter or margarine

Parsley sprig

1. Combine eggs, salt, and 1 tablespoon cold water in small bowl; beat, with rotary beater, just until combined, not frothy.

2. Combine rest of ingredients, except butter and the parsley sprig. Stir the combined ingredients into eggs, mixing well.

3. Slowly heat a medium-size, heavy skillet. It is ready when small amount of cold water sprinkled over surface sizzles and rolls off in drops. Add butter; heat until it sizzles briskly (not browned).

4. Quickly turn egg mixture into skillet; cook over medium heat. As the omelet sets, loosen the edge with spatula, and tilt skillet, to let the uncooked egg mixture run under set portion.

5. When omelet is dry on top and golden brown on bottom, fold it over to edge of pan. Tilt out onto hot serving plate. Serve the omelet at once, garnished with parsley sprig.

Makes 1 or 2 servings.

Note: Or substitute dried herbs for fresh, using half the quantity.

HAM-AND-CHEESE OMELET

Filling

2 teaspoons butter or margarine
½ cup cubed cooked ham
½ teaspoon instant minced onion
1 can (3 ounces) chopped mushrooms, drained

2 teaspoons chopped parsley
⅓ cup cubed sharp Cheddar cheese

Omelet

6 eggs
¼ teaspoon seasoned salt
Dash pepper

1½ tablespoons butter or margarine

Chopped parsley

1. Make Filling: In hot butter in small skillet, sauté ham, onion, mushrooms, and parsley, stirring, 5 minutes. Remove from heat.
2. Add cheese cubes. Cover, and keep warm.
3. Make Omelet: In medium-size bowl, with wire whisk or rotary beater, beat eggs, seasoned salt, pepper, and 1 tablespoon cold water just until combined but not frothy.
4. Meanwhile, slowly heat a 9-inch skillet or omelet pan. Add butter; heat until it sizzles briskly—it should not brown.
5. Turn omelet mixture all at once into skillet; cook, over medium heat.
6. As omelet sets, run spatula around edge to loosen; tilt pan to let uncooked portion run underneath.
7. Continue loosening and tilting until omelet is almost dry on top and golden brown underneath.
8. Spoon warm filling down center of omelet; fold in half. Tilt out onto heated platter. Sprinkle with parsley.

Makes 4 servings.

OMELETS MADE TO ORDER

Basic Omelet

16 eggs
½ cup light cream
2 teaspoons salt
Dash pepper

Fillings (see pp. 65–67)
½ cup butter or margarine

1. Make Basic Omelet: In large bowl, with electric mixer at low speed or with rotary beater, beat eggs with cream, salt, and pepper until well blended but not frothy. Refrigerate the mixture until you are ready to cook omelets.
2. Make the Fillings.

3. To cook omelet: Slowly heat an 8-inch skillet. Add 1 tablespoon butter, and heat until it sizzles briskly but does not brown.

4. Ladle about ½ cup egg mixture into skillet; cook over medium heat. As egg sets, run spatula around edge to loosen, and tilt pan to let uncooked portion run underneath. Continue loosening and tilting until the omelet is almost dry on top and golden brown underneath.

5. Place your choice of filling on half of omelet. Fold other half over, and slide omelet onto heated serving plate.

Makes 8 omelets.

RED-CAVIAR-AND-SOUR-CREAM FILLING

1 jar (4 ounces) red caviar	1 cup (½ pint) dairy sour cream

1. Turn caviar and sour cream into small bowls.

2. Spread omelet, still in skillet, with 3 tablespoons sour cream.

3. Fold over omelet; slide onto serving plate, and top with a heaping teaspoonful of drained red caviar. Serve omelet at once.

Makes enough for 4 or 5 omelets.

CREAMED-OYSTER FILLING

1 can (8 ounces) oysters	1 tablespoon chopped shallot
Milk	or onion
2 tablespoons butter or	3 tablespoons flour
margarine	

1. Drain liquid from oysters into 1-cup measure; add milk to make 1 cup.

2. In hot butter in small saucepan, sauté shallot until tender—about 2 minutes. Remove from heat. Stir in flour until well combined. Gradually stir in milk mixture. Bring to boil, stirring constantly; reduce heat, and simmer 1 minute.

3. Add oysters; return to boil. Turn into serving bowl; keep warm.

Makes enough for 4 omelets (¼ cup each).

CREAMED-SPINACH FILLING

1 package (10 ounces) frozen leaf spinach
1 tablespoon butter or margarine
1 tablespoon flour
1 cup light cream
⅛ teaspoon nutmeg

1. Cook spinach as package label directs. Drain well; chop.
2. Melt butter in small saucepan; remove from heat. Stir in flour until smooth; gradually stir in cream; add nutmeg. Bring to boil, stirring constantly; reduce heat, and simmer 1 minute. Stir in spinach. Turn into serving bowl; keep warm.

Makes enough for 4 to 6 omelets (about ⅓ cup each).

MUENSTER-CHEESE-WITH-CARAWAY FILLING

½ cup grated Muenster cheese
1 teaspoon caraway seed

1. Combine cheese and caraway in serving bowl.
Makes enough for 4 omelets (2 tablespoons each).

CHICKEN-LIVER-AND-MUSHROOM FILLING

½ pound chicken livers
3 tablespoons butter or margarine
¼ pound mushrooms, chopped
1 teaspoon instant minced onion
½ teaspoon seasoned salt
¼ teaspoon dried chervil leaves
⅛ teaspoon pepper
⅓ cup dry sherry

1. Rinse chicken livers; pat dry with paper towels. Cut into small pieces.
2. In hot butter in medium-size saucepan, sauté mushrooms until golden brown—about 2 minutes. Add liver, onion, seasoned salt, chervil,

and pepper; sauté until liver is browned—about 4 minutes. Add sherry; reduce heat, and simmer 5 minutes. Turn into serving bowl; keep warm.
Makes enough for 4 to 6 omelets (about ⅓ cup each).

PUFFY OMELET WITH CHERRY PRESERVES

6 egg whites	2 tablespoons butter or
⅛ teaspoon cream of tartar	margarine
6 egg yolks	2 teaspoons salad oil
¾ teaspoon salt	
Dash pepper	Confectioners' sugar
6 tablespoons milk	Cherry preserves

1. In large bowl of electric mixer, let egg whites warm to room temperature—about 1 hour.

2. At high speed, beat egg whites with cream of tartar just until stiff peaks form when beater is slowly raised.

3. In small bowl of electric mixer, using same beater, beat egg yolks until thick and lemon-colored.

4. Add salt, pepper, and milk gradually; beat until well combined.

5. With wire whisk or rubber scraper, using an under-and-over motion, gently fold egg-yolk mixture into egg whites just until combined.

6. Slowly heat a 9- or 10-inch heavy skillet with a heat-resistant handle, or an omelet pan. To test temperature: Sprinkle a little cold water on skillet; water should sizzle and roll off in drops.

7. Add butter and oil; heat until butter mixture sizzles briskly—it should not brown. Tilt pan to coat side with butter mixture.

8. Spread egg mixture evenly in pan; cook, over low heat and without stirring, until lightly browned on underside—about 10 minutes. Meanwhile, preheat oven to 350°F.

9. Transfer skillet to oven; bake omelet 10 to 15 minutes, or until top seems firm when gently pressed with fingertip.

10. To serve: Fold omelet in half. Turn out onto heated serving platter. Sprinkle with confectioners' sugar. Serve with cherry preserves.
Makes 4 to 6 servings.

SPINACH-AND-SOUR-CREAM OMELET

Filling

1 package (10 ounces) frozen
   chopped spinach
⅓ cup dairy sour cream

½ teaspoon salt
⅛ teaspoon nutmeg

Omelet

6 eggs
½ teaspoon salt
Dash pepper
1½ tablespoons butter or
    margarine

Sour cream

1. Make Filling: Cook spinach as package label directs; drain well.

2. Add ⅓ cup sour cream, ½ teaspoon salt, and nutmeg. Cover, and keep warm.

3. Make Omelet: In medium-size bowl, with wire whisk or rotary beater, beat eggs, salt, pepper, and 1 tablespoon cold water just until combined but not frothy.

4. Meanwhile, slowly heat 9-inch skillet or omelet pan. Add butter; heat until it sizzles briskly—it should not brown.

5. Turn omelet mixture all at once into skillet; cook, over medium heat.

6. As omelet sets, run spatula around edge to loosen; tilt pan to let uncooked portion run underneath.

7. Continue loosening and tilting until omelet is almost dry on top and golden brown underneath.

8. Spoon warm filling down center of omelet; fold in half. Tilt out onto heated platter.

9. Top with additional sour cream.

Makes 4 servings.

HAM-AND-EGG ROULADE

Ham Filling

1 pound ground cooked ham (2 cups)	1 cup mayonnaise or cooked salad dressing
1 cup chopped celery	

Roulade

4 eggs	⅛ teaspoon dried thyme leaves
¼ cup butter or margarine	2 cups milk
½ cup unsifted all-purpose flour	
¾ teaspoon salt	Cheddar-Cheese Sauce (see
⅛ teaspoon pepper	p. 70)

1. Make Ham Filling: In 1-quart casserole, combine ham, celery, and mayonnaise; mix well. Set aside, covered, until ready to bake.

2. Make Roulade: Preheat oven to 325°F. Grease a 15½- by 10½- by 1-inch jelly-roll pan. Line with waxed paper; grease and flour paper.

3. Separate eggs, placing the whites in a large bowl and the yolks in a medium-size bowl.

4. Melt butter in medium-size saucepan; remove from heat. Stir in flour, salt, pepper, and thyme until smooth. Gradually stir in milk; bring to boil, stirring constantly. Reduce heat, and simmer, stirring, until mixture becomes very thick—about 1 minute. Remove from heat.

5. With wire whisk or wooden spoon, beat egg yolks. Gradually beat in cooked mixture.

6. With electric mixer at high speed, beat egg whites just until stiff peaks form when beater is slowly raised.

7. With wire whisk or rubber scraper, fold egg-yolk mixture into egg whites just until blended. Turn into prepared pan; spread evenly.

8. Bake roulade 45 to 50 minutes, or until it is golden brown and top springs back when lightly pressed with fingertip. Bake ham filling in oven at same time as roulade.

9. Meanwhile, make Cheddar-Cheese Sauce. Keep warm.

10. Loosen edge of roulade with spatula; top with oiled sheet of waxed paper; then top with cookie sheet. Quickly invert; lift off jelly-roll pan, and peel off waxed-paper lining.

11. Stir filling; spoon evenly over roulade. Starting from short side, roll up, using waxed paper as guide. Turn onto serving platter. Serve with sauce.

Makes 6 to 8 servings.

CHEDDAR-CHEESE SAUCE

3 tablespoons butter or margarine
3 tablespoons flour
¼ teaspoon dry mustard
1 teaspoon Worcestershire sauce

½ teaspoon salt
2 cups milk
1 package (8 ounces) sharp Cheddar cheese, grated
1 tablespoon chopped parsley

1. Melt butter in medium-size saucepan. Remove from heat. Stir in flour, mustard, Worcestershire, and salt until smooth. Gradually stir in milk.

2. Bring to boil, stirring; boil 1 minute.

3. Remove from heat. Add cheese and parsley, stirring until all the cheese is melted.

4. Serve over Ham-and-Egg Roulade.

Makes about 2⅔ cups.

CHICKEN SOUFFLÉ HOLLANDAISE

6 egg whites
¼ cup butter or margarine
¼ cup unsifted all-purpose flour
1 teaspoon salt
Dash pepper
1 cup milk

¼ teaspoon cream of tartar
4 egg yolks
1¼ cups finely chopped cooked chicken

Hollandaise Sauce (see p. 60)

1. Preheat oven to 375°F.

2. In large bowl of electric mixer, let egg whites warm to room temperature.

3. Melt butter in medium-size saucepan; remove from heat. Stir in flour, salt, and pepper until smooth; then stir in milk.

4. Over medium heat, bring to boiling point, stirring. Remove the saucepan from heat; let the sauce cool for 10 minutes.

5. With mixer at high speed, beat egg whites with cream of tartar just until stiff peaks form when beater is slowly raised.

6. In small bowl of mixer, beat the egg yolks until they are light and fluffy.

7. Into cooled sauce, stir chicken, then egg yolks. With wire whisk or rubber scraper, gently fold into egg whites, using under-and-over motion. Turn into ungreased 2-quart, straight-sided soufflé dish.

8. Make top hat: With back of large spoon, make a deep path around the soufflé top, about 1 inch from edge. Set dish in pan containing about 1 inch hot water; bake 55 to 60 minutes.

9. About 15 minutes before soufflé is done, make Hollandaise Sauce. Serve at once.

Makes 6 servings.

PARMESAN-CHEESE SOUFFLÉ WITH ONION SAUCE

5 egg whites	1 teaspoon salt
¼ cup butter or margarine	¼ teaspoon pepper
¼ cup unsifted all-purpose flour	5 egg yolks, slightly beaten
1 cup milk	
1 cup freshly grated Parmesan cheese	Onion Sauce (see p. 72)

1. In large bowl of electric mixer, let egg whites warm to room temperature—about 1 hour.

2. Meanwhile, preheat oven to 375°F.

3. Slowly heat butter in small saucepan; remove from heat. Stir in flour until smooth. Gradually stir in milk.

4. Cook, stirring, over medium heat, until mixture begins to boil. Remove from heat.

5. Add cheese, salt, and pepper, mixing well. Let cool; then stir in egg yolks.

6. With mixer at high speed, beat egg whites until stiff peaks form when beater is slowly raised.

7. With wire whisk or rubber scraper, gently fold cheese mixture into the egg whites. Turn into an ungreased 1½-quart straight-sided soufflé dish.

8. Make top hat: With back of large spoon, make a deep path around top of soufflé, 1 inch from edge of dish.

9. Bake 35 minutes, or until top is golden brown. Serve at once, with Onion Sauce.

Makes 4 servings.

ONION SAUCE

5 tablespoons butter or margarine	1 package (1¾ ounces) dried onion-soup mix
3 tablespoons flour	2½ cups milk

1. Slowly heat butter in medium-size saucepan; remove from heat. Stir in flour and soup mix.

2. Gradually stir in milk; bring to boil, stirring. Reduce heat; simmer 1 minute. Pass sauce along with soufflé.

Makes 2½ cups.

SALMON SOUFFLÉ WITH OYSTER SAUCE

6 egg whites	6 egg yolks, slightly beaten
1 tablespoon flour	1 can (10½ ounces) condensed cream-of-mushroom soup, undiluted
1 teaspoon dry mustard	
Dash salt	
¼ teaspoon pepper	1 can (7¾ ounces) salmon, drained and flaked
1 teaspoon Worcestershire sauce	⅛ teaspoon cream of tartar

Sauce

1	can (7 ounces) frozen oysters, thawed	1	cup milk
2	tablespoons butter or margarine	½	teaspoon salt
		⅛	teaspoon pepper
2	tablespoons flour	1½	tablespoons lemon juice

1. In large bowl of electric mixer, let egg whites warm to room temperature—about 1 hour.

2. Meanwhile, preheat oven to 350°F. Lightly grease a 1½-quart straight-sided soufflé dish.

3. In medium-size saucepan, combine flour, mustard, salt, pepper, and Worcestershire. Gradually stir in egg yolks and soup until smooth.

4. Cook, stirring constantly, over very low heat, 8 to 10 minutes, or until mixture is thickened and smooth.

5. Remove from heat. Add salmon, mixing well. Let cool slightly.

6. At high speed, beat egg whites with cream of tartar until stiff peaks form when beater is slowly raised.

7. With wire whisk or rubber scraper, gently fold salmon mixture into egg whites just until combined.

8. Turn into prepared soufflé dish. Set dish in pan containing 1 inch hot water; bake 1 hour.

9. Meanwhile, make Sauce: Drain oysters, reserving ½ cup liquid. Cut oysters into thirds.

10. Melt butter in small saucepan. Remove from heat. Stir in flour until smooth. Gradually stir in liquid from oysters and the milk.

11. Cook, stirring, over medium heat, until mixture begins to boil and is thickened.

12. Stir in salt, pepper, and oysters; reheat gently.

13. Just before serving, stir in lemon juice. Serve sauce along with soufflé.

Makes 4 to 6 servings.

SPINACH SOUFFLÉ

6   eggs
½   pound spinach
5   tablespoons butter or
    margarine
6   tablespoons all-purpose flour
1¼ cups milk

⅓   cup grated Swiss cheese
1   tablespoon chopped parsley
¼   teaspoon garlic salt
⅛   teaspoon pepper
½   teaspoon salt
¼   teaspoon cream of tartar

1. Separate eggs, placing whites in large bowl of electric mixer and yolks in another large bowl.

2. Fold a 26-inch-long piece of waxed paper lengthwise into thirds. Lightly butter one side. Wrap around a 1½-quart straight-sided soufflé dish (7½-inch diameter), buttered side against dish, to form a collar extending 2 inches above top; tie with string.

3. Wash spinach; remove and discard stems. Place in large saucepan with ½ cup water; bring to boil. Boil gently, covered, 5 minutes, or just until tender. Drain well. Chop finely; makes ¾ cup.

4. Melt butter in medium-size saucepan; remove from heat. Stir in flour until smooth. Gradually stir in milk.

5. Bring to boil, stirring constantly. Reduce heat, and simmer, stirring, about 1 minute, or until mixture becomes very thick and begins to leave bottom and sides of pan. Remove from heat.

6. With wire whisk or wooden spoon, beat egg yolks; beat in cooked mixture. Add chopped spinach, cheese, parsley, garlic salt, and pepper; beat until well combined.

7. Add salt and cream of tartar to egg whites. With electric beater at high speed, beat until stiff peaks form when beater is slowly raised. Fold one third into warm spinach mixture until well combined. Carefully fold in remaining egg whites just until combined.

8. Turn into prepared dish. Refrigerate until baking time—no longer than 4 hours. (See note.)

9. About 65 minutes before serving, preheat oven to 350°F. Bake soufflé about 50 minutes, or until puffed and golden brown. Remove waxed paper, and serve soufflé at once.

Makes 6 to 8 servings.

Note: If desired, soufflé may be baked at once, without refrigerating, about 35 minutes.

SWISS-CHEESE SOUFFLÉ IN CREAM-PUFF SHELL

Cream-Puff Shell

¼ cup butter or margarine
⅛ teaspoon salt

½ cup sifted all-purpose flour
2 eggs

Soufflé

6 eggs
5 tablespoons butter or
   margarine
6 tablespoons unsifted
   all-purpose flour
Salt

Dash cayenne
1¼ cups milk
½ cup coarsely grated natural
   Swiss cheese (2 ounces)
½ cup grated Parmesan cheese
¼ teaspoon cream of tartar

1. Make Cream-Puff Shell: In medium-size saucepan, bring ½ cup water, the butter, and salt to boil. Remove from heat. With wooden spoon, beat in flour all at once.

2. Return to low heat; continue beating until mixture forms ball and leaves sides of pan. Remove from heat.

3. Beat in 2 eggs, one at a time, beating hard after each addition until mixture is smooth. Continue beating until dough is shiny and satiny and breaks in strands.

4. Turn dough into ungreased, deep, 10-inch pie plate with fluted edge. Spread evenly over bottom and sides of dish. Set aside while preparing soufflé.

5. Preheat oven to 425°F.

6. Make Soufflé: Separate 6 eggs, placing whites in large bowl, yolks in medium-size bowl.

7. Melt butter in small saucepan; remove from heat. Stir in flour, 1 teaspoon salt, and the cayenne until smooth. Gradually stir in milk.

8. Bring to boil, stirring. Reduce heat, and simmer, stirring, until mixture becomes very thick—about 1 minute. Remove from heat.

9. With wire whisk or wooden spoon, beat egg yolks. Gradually beat in cooked mixture. Add both cheeses; beat until well combined.

10. Add ½ teaspoon salt and the cream of tartar to egg whites. With electric mixer at high speed, beat just until stiff peaks form when beater is slowly raised.

11. With wire whisk or rubber scraper, fold one third of beaten egg whites into cheese mixture. Carefully fold in remaining egg whites just until blended. Turn into Cream-Puff Shell.

12. Bake 20 minutes. Reduce heat to 350°F. and bake 20 minutes longer.

13. Serve immediately, cut in wedges.

Makes 6 to 8 servings.

4

BRUNCH FAVORITES

The recipes collected under the title "Brunch Favorites" run the gamut from pancakes, fritters, and crêpes to fondue. No matter what type of brunch you have planned, you will find in the following pages a selection of excellent main dishes or companions to the main course.

Throughout modern history, thin cakes made with batter—pancakes, fritters, crêpes, blintzes, waffles—have been relished by persons of all ages. No doubt these recipes, brought to this country by the European settlers, were especially popular with farm workers and frontiersmen, who required hearty food and lots of it to give them enough physical energy to carry out their daily labors. The Pennsylvania Dutch share in this hearty tradition. Their pancakes, made with buckwheat flour, corn meal, and dark, unrefined molasses, merit the reputation they have earned.

The batters for these dishes are quite simple to prepare, but there are several tricks to making *pancakes* that will ensure perfect results. The first is to barely mix the batter: Using a long-handled wooden spoon, stir the mixture until it is only slightly moistened. The batter will be lumpy. If you want even fluffier pancakes, allow the batter to sit, covered, for several hours. Then if the batter seems too thick, add a small amount of water; if too thin, a bit of flour.

If you are cooking the pancakes in a skillet, grease it lightly before starting each new batch. A soapstone griddle will not require greasing if there are several tablespoons of oil or butter in your recipe. In either case, bring the utensil to a high temperature slowly. If you need to oil your pan, place the oil in it before you begin to heat it. A good rule to follow in the kitchen is never to place empty utensils on heating sources. Test for the proper temperature by splattering a few drops of cold water onto the skillet surface. If it has reached the required temperature, the water will bounce and sizzle. If it evaporates, the cooking surface is too hot.

When your griddle is ready, pour several pools of pancake batter onto it. Allow them to cook until the bubbles that appear on the surface begin to break. With a wide pancake turner, gently flip them to the other side to cook for another minute or two. Avoid turning your pancakes more than once since each turning toughens them. If you cannot serve them immediately, separate them with pieces of cloth and keep them warm in a very low oven.

For a pleasant variation, add fruit or nuts to the batter. Blueberries and pecans are traditional, but you can experiment with other berries and nuts or add some crunchy wheat germ for a nutritional boost and a delicious, nutlike flavor. Top with pure maple syrup, thick country-store molasses, or seafood. Or spread applesauce or marmalade, sprinkled with cinnamon, between layers of pancakes and top with vanilla ice cream or sweetened whipped cream. The possibilities are endless.

Waffle batter should also be mixed very lightly. Follow manufacturer's directions given with your waffle iron for proper baking. It should need no greasing. Simply heat it to the required temperature and fill two-thirds full with batter. When steam ceases to escape from the cracks in the waffle iron and its lid, the waffle is probably ready. However, if the lid resists opening, allow it to cook another minute or so. Waffles may be served in different styles; you can fill them more easily than you can pancakes and crêpes because of their crisp texture. Vary the basic recipe for French Waffles given in this book by adding raisins, nuts, or coconut. A topping of blueberries, whole or mashed and sweetened, with vanilla ice cream makes a good company dessert. Or omit the sugar and add one-half cup grated cheese and perhaps chopped ham or bacon.

Fritter batters are best when they have had a chance to rest, covered and refrigerated, for at least several hours. Make certain that the food you intend to cook with this mixture is as dry as possible so that the batter will hold up when the other food is added. If you are incorporating uncooked meat, mince it before adding it to your fritter. You might try making fruit fritters, using almost any fruit that has been cut into wedges. Marinate it first in kirsch, brandy, or rum, drain it, and roll the wedges in confectioners' sugar before adding to the fritter batter.

The other favorites included in this section are simple to prepare and make marvelous brunch dishes. *Quiche,* for example, has always been associated with elegant dining, but the recipe included here for Quiche Tartlets is simple enough to prepare for even a family brunch. *French Toast,* doused with maple syrup or garnished with any of the other toppings mentioned above, is another well-loved food.

A recipe for Swiss Fondue has also been included, since the dish lends itself so readily to brunch menus. It can be served in an informal, buffet style if you wish, or it can be prepared in an elegant copper chafing dish, to take its place in the center of the most elegant table. See the Menu chapter for accompaniments.

BANANA GRIDDLECAKES

2 cups packaged pancake mix	Butter or margarine, melted
Milk	
Eggs	Butter
Salad oil	Maple syrup
3 bananas	

1. Make pancake mix with milk, eggs, and salad oil as package label directs.

2. Slice bananas ⅛ inch thick.

3. Heat griddle or large skillet over medium heat. Brush lightly with some of the melted butter.

4. For each griddlecake, arrange 4 or 5 banana slices within a 3-inch circle on griddle. Ladle ¼ cup batter over slices.

5. Cook until bubbles form on surface and bottom is golden brown. Turn carefully; cook 2 minutes longer, or until browned on the underside. Brush griddle with butter as needed.

6. Serve with butter and hot maple syrup.

Makes 18 griddlecakes; 6 servings.

BLUEBERRY OR STRAWBERRY PANCAKES

1¾ cups unsifted all-purpose
    flour
3 tablespoons sugar
4 teaspoons baking powder
¾ teaspoon salt
1¾ cups milk
2 eggs

3 tablespoons salad oil
1½ cups blueberries, washed and
    drained, or 1 pint strawberries,
    washed, hulled, sliced

Butter
Syrup

1. Sift flour, sugar, baking powder, and salt into medium-size bowl.
2. In another medium-size bowl, combine milk, eggs, and oil; mix well with fork. Add to flour mixture; stir just until combined—batter will be lumpy.
3. Meanwhile, slowly heat griddle or electric skillet to 350°F., or until a little cold water, dropped on griddle, rolls off in drops.
4. Ladle batter (about ¼ cupful) onto hot griddle. Sprinkle each pancake with 2 to 3 tablespoons blueberries or strawberries. Cook until bubbles form on surface and edges become dry. Turn, and cook 2 minutes longer, or until nicely browned on underside.
5. Serve hot, with butter and maple, blueberry, or strawberry syrup. Makes 12 (4-inch) pancakes.

BUTTERMILK PANCAKES WITH STRAWBERRIES AND SOUR CREAM

2 pints fresh strawberries

Pancakes
1 egg
1¾ cups milk
1½ cups buttermilk-pancake mix
2 tablespoons butter or
    margarine, melted

3 tablespoons sugar
1 cup dairy sour cream

1. Prepare strawberries: Wash, drain, and hull strawberries. Cut in halves into medium-size bowl. Let stand at room temperature.

2. Make Pancakes: In medium-size bowl, beat together egg and milk. Stir in pancake mix just until batter is smooth. Stir in butter.

3. Meanwhile, heat griddle or heavy skillet. To test temperature, drop a little cold water onto griddle; water should roll off in drops.

4. Use about ⅓ cup batter for each pancake. (Pancakes should be about 6 inches across.) Cook until bubbles form on surface and edge becomes dry. Turn; cook 2 minutes, or until browned on underside.

5. Sprinkle strawberries with sugar; mix gently.

6. Place a pancake on a serving plate; top with about ½ cup strawberries; fold over pancake; fasten with a decorative wooden pick. Top with heaping tablespoon sour cream.

Makes 8 servings.

POTATO PANCAKES

4 large potatoes	½ teaspoon pepper
1 onion, grated	2 eggs, beaten
3 to 4 tablespoons all-purpose flour or pancake mix	Chicken fat or butter
1 teaspoon salt	Applesauce (optional)

1. Wash and peel potatoes. Grate them on coarse grater, and drain well on paper towels.

2. Mix drained potato with onion, flour, salt, pepper, and eggs.

3. Heat a little chicken fat or butter in skillet; drop batter by heaping tablespoonfuls into fat and fry until pancakes are well browned on both sides (3 to 4 minutes each side).

4. Serve hot, with applesauce, if desired.

Makes about 8 pancakes.

RUSSIAN PANCAKES

Batter

6 tablespoons butter or
  margarine
½ cup unsifted all-purpose flour
½ cup light cream
3 eggs, separated
1 teaspoon grated lemon peel

¾ cup apricot preserves
Confectioners' sugar

Whipped cream (optional)

1. Make Batter: In medium-size saucepan, combine 4 tablespoons butter and ½ cup water; heat to boiling.

2. Remove from heat. With wooden spoon, beat in flour. Return to low heat; beat until mixture forms a ball and leaves sides of pan.

3. Remove from heat; beat in cream. Add egg yolks, one at a time, beating well after each addition. Stir in lemon peel.

4. In medium-size bowl, beat egg whites until stiff peaks form when beater is raised.

5. Add one third of egg whites to egg-yolk mixture; stir until completely mixed. With wire whisk or rubber spatula, fold in remaining egg whites just until blended. Set batter aside until ready to make pancakes.

6. When ready to serve, make pancakes: Heat a 6- or 8-inch heavy skillet. Add ½ tablespoon butter (butter should sizzle but not brown); tip skillet to coat bottom.

7. Pour about ¾ cup batter into skillet; quickly spread into a 6-inch circle. Cook over low heat 4 or 5 minutes, or until golden brown on underside; turn, and brown other side. Remove; keep warm. Repeat with remaining batter and butter, to make 4 pancakes. At the same time, heat apricot preserves.

8. To serve: Stack pancakes, on heated serving plate, spreading hot apricot preserves between them. Sprinkle top with confectioners' sugar. Serve at once, with whipped cream, if desired.

Makes 4 servings.

Note: If you like, you may make the batter an hour or so ahead of time. Let stand at room temperature. Then make the pancakes just before serving.

SURPRISE PANCAKES

1 cup milk	½ cup raisins
1 egg	
1 tablespoon salad oil	Butter or margarine
1 cup packaged pancake mix	Hot maple syrup or honey
½ cup wheat germ	

1. Heat griddle; grease very lightly.
2. In medium-size bowl, with rotary beater, beat milk with egg and oil just until combined.
3. Stir in pancake mix, wheat germ, and raisins.
4. Use ¼ cup batter for each pancake. Cook pancakes until lightly browned—about 3 minutes on a side.
5. Serve with butter and maple syrup or honey.
Makes 8 medium-size pancakes.

FRENCH TOAST

4 slices white bread, ¾ inch thick	Confectioners' sugar or cinnamon-sugar
3 eggs	
¾ cup milk	Bacon (optional)
1 tablespoon granulated sugar	Maple syrup (optional)
¼ teaspoon salt	Strawberries (optional)
2 tablespoons butter or margarine	

1. Arrange bread in single layer in 9-inch-square baking dish.
2. In small bowl, with rotary beater, beat eggs, milk, granulated sugar, and salt until blended. Pour over bread; turn slices to coat evenly.
3. Refrigerate, covered, overnight, or at least 4 hours.
4. In hot butter in skillet, sauté bread until golden—about 4 minutes on each side. Sprinkle with confectioners' sugar or cinnamon-sugar, and serve with bacon and syrup, if desired. Or serve with sliced strawberries.
Makes 4 servings.

PAIN PERDU

2 eggs
½ cup granulated sugar
1 cup milk
1 teaspoon vanilla extract
½ teaspoon grated lemon peel
8 slices day-old French bread (1 inch thick)
2 tablespoons butter or margarine

Confectioners' sugar
Nutmeg

Preserves or syrup (optional)

1. In small bowl, with rotary beater, beat eggs with granulated sugar. Stir in milk, vanilla, and lemon peel.
2. Arrange bread in single layer in shallow dish. Pour egg mixture over slices. Let stand 30 minutes.
3. In hot butter in large skillet, sauté bread until golden brown—about 6 minutes per side.
4. Arrange on serving platter. Sprinkle with confectioners' sugar and nutmeg. Serve with preserves or syrup, if desired.

Makes 4 servings.

FRENCH WAFFLES

1½ cups sifted all-purpose flour
2 teaspoons baking powder
½ teaspoon salt
3 eggs
1 tablespoon sugar
1½ cups milk

⅓ cup butter or margarine, melted

Butter
Maple syrup

1. Preheat waffle iron as manufacturer directs.
2. Sift flour with baking powder and salt. Set aside.
3. Separate eggs, placing whites in small bowl, yolks in medium-size bowl.
4. With electric mixer, beat egg whites with sugar just until stiff peaks form when beater is slowly raised. Set aside.

5. Using same beater, beat egg yolks until light. Add milk and melted butter; beat until well combined.

6. At low speed, beat in flour mixture just until smooth. With rubber scraper, fold in egg whites just until combined.

7. Bake waffles, as manufacturer directs, until golden. Serve hot, with butter and warm syrup.

Makes 3 large or 4 medium-size waffles.

CORN CAKES WITH BACON

About 12 bacon slices, halved crosswise
1¼ cups sifted all-purpose flour
2 teaspoons baking powder
1 teaspoon salt
⅛ teaspoon pepper

2 eggs, slightly beaten
1 cup milk
1 can (12 ounces) whole-kernel corn, drained

Maple syrup

1. Sauté bacon in skillet. Drain, reserving ½ cup drippings.

2. Into medium-size bowl, sift flour, baking powder, salt, and pepper.

3. Combine eggs, milk, and 3 tablespoons reserved drippings; mix well. Turn into flour mixture; beat until well mixed. Stir in corn.

4. Meanwhile, slowly heat griddle or heavy skillet. To test temperature: Sprinkle a little cold water over griddle; water should roll off in drops.

5. Drop batter by heaping tablespoonfuls onto ungreased griddle. (If using skillet, grease with remaining bacon drippings.)

6. Cook, over low heat, until underside is browned. Turn; brown other side.

7. Serve cakes hot, with maple syrup and bacon.

Makes 4 to 6 servings.

FRIED CORNMEAL MUSH

1 cup cornmeal
1 teaspoon salt
1 teaspoon sugar

½ pound bacon slices

Maple syrup or honey

1. In medium-size saucepan, bring 3 cups water to boil.

2. In 2-cup measure, combine 1 cup cold water, the cornmeal, salt, and sugar; stir until combined.

3. Gradually add to boiling water, stirring briskly. Cook, stirring frequently, until thickened; then cook over low heat, covered, 10 minutes.

4. Pour into 8½- by 4½- by 2⅝-inch loaf pan. Cool; refrigerate, covered, until well chilled—overnight.

5. At serving time, fry bacon until crisp. Drain, and keep warm. Reserve drippings.

6. Turn cornmeal mush onto board; cut crosswise into 12 slices.

7. Lightly grease a hot griddle with reserved bacon drippings. Add cornmeal slices, and cook over medium heat until lightly browned on each side—6 to 8 minutes per side. Serve with bacon and syrup or honey.

Makes 4 servings.

FETA-CHEESE PIE

½ package (10-ounce size) piecrust mix
3 tablespoons butter or margarine
3 tablespoons flour
1½ cups milk
½ pound feta cheese, at room temperature
3 eggs
¼ cup chopped parsley

1. Prepare piecrust mix as package label directs. Shape into a ball. On lightly floured surface, roll out pastry into an 11-inch square.

2. Fit into an 8- by 8- by 2-inch baking pan. Fold pastry under about ⅜ inch, and flute edges. Refrigerate until ready to use.

3. Preheat oven to 350°F.

4. Melt butter in small saucepan; remove from heat. Stir in flour until smooth. Gradually stir in milk.

5. Bring to boil, stirring constantly. Reduce heat, and simmer 1 minute. Remove sauce from heat.

6. Crumble cheese into medium-size bowl; with electric mixer, beat until smooth. Gradually beat in sauce.

7. Add eggs; beat just until combined. Stir in parsley. Pour into pie shell.

8. Bake 45 minutes, or until filling feels firm when pressed with fingertip. Serve warm.

Makes 8 appetizer servings.

CORN-HAM FRITTATA WITH CHEESE SAUCE

6 eggs	1 cup chopped cooked ham
½ teaspoon salt	2 tablespoons butter or
½ teaspoon dried thyme leaves	margarine
1 cup drained canned	
whole-kernel corn	Cheese Sauce (see below)

1. In medium-size bowl, with rotary beater, beat 3 eggs, ¼ teaspoon salt, ¼ teaspoon thyme, and 1 tablespoon cold water; beat until well combined but not frothy.

2. Stir in ½ cup corn, ½ cup ham.

3. Slowly heat a heavy 9-inch skillet or omelet pan.

4. Add 1 tablespoon butter to skillet; heat until it sizzles briskly. Turn egg mixture into skillet; cook, over medium heat, until golden underneath. As frittata sets, run spatula around edge, to loosen; tilt pan to let uncooked portion run under.

5. When almost dry on top, run under broiler, 6 inches from heat, till top is set and golden—about 2 minutes. Tilt out onto plate; keep warm.

6. Repeat directions, to make another frittata. Serve hot, with Cheese Sauce.

Makes 4 servings.

CHEESE SAUCE

1 can (11 ounces) condensed	¼ cup milk
Cheddar-cheese soup,	2 teaspoons brown sugar
undiluted	1 teaspoon prepared mustard

1. In small saucepan, blend soup and milk until smooth. Add brown sugar and mustard, mixing well.

2. Cook, over medium heat, stirring, until sauce is hot. Serve with Corn-Ham Frittata.

Makes 1½ cups.

ONION-POTATO FRITTATA

2 tablespoons butter or margarine
⅓ cup thinly sliced onion
1 cup diced, pared raw potato
6 eggs

1 teaspoon seasoned salt
Dash dried thyme leaves
1 tablespoon finely chopped parsley

1. Slowly melt butter in a 9-inch heavy skillet or omelet pan with heat-resistant handle.

2. Add onion and potato; sauté, stirring, 8 to 10 minutes, or until potato is tender.

3. Meanwhile, with rotary beater, beat eggs with 2 tablespoons water, the salt, thyme, and parsley just until combined, not frothy.

4. Pour egg mixture over onion and potato. Cook over low heat. As eggs set, lift with spatula to let uncooked portion run underneath.

5. When eggs are almost set on top, run under broiler, 6 inches from heat, 2 to 3 minutes, or until golden.

6. Turn out, without folding, onto heated serving platter.

Makes 4 servings.

SWISS-CHEESE FRITTERS

Salad oil or shortening for deep-frying
2 cups grated natural Swiss cheese (½ pound)
¼ cup unsifted all-purpose flour

1 teaspoon salt
½ teaspoon pepper
4 egg whites
¼ cup packaged dry bread crumbs

1. In deep skillet or deep-fat fryer, slowly heat salad oil or shortening (at least 2 inches) to 375°F. on deep-frying thermometer.

2. Combine cheese, flour, salt, and pepper on sheet of waxed paper.

3. In medium-size bowl, beat egg whites until stiff peaks form when beater is slowly raised. Gently fold cheese mixture into the beaten egg whites until well combined.

4. Shape by tablespoonfuls into 1-inch balls; roll in bread crumbs.

5. Deep-fry a few at a time, turning once, 1 minute, or until golden brown on both sides. Drain on paper towels.

6. Serve hot, on wooden picks, with a salad, if desired.

Makes 22 fritters, or about 5 servings.

Note: For convenience in serving, these fritters may be fried, then frozen or refrigerated. Heat on a cookie sheet, in oven preheated to 400°F.—5 minutes for refrigerated fritters, 7 minutes for frozen.

VIENNA-SAUSAGE FRITTERS

1 cup sifted all-purpose flour
1½ teaspoons double-acting baking powder
½ teaspoon salt
1 teaspoon dry mustard
1 egg, separated
½ cup milk

1 tablespoon salad oil
Salad oil or shortening for deep-frying
3 cans (4-ounce size) Vienna sausages

Sharp prepared mustard

1. Sift flour with baking powder, salt, and mustard.

2. In small bowl, with rotary beater, beat egg white until stiff peaks form.

3. In another small bowl, with same beater, beat egg yolk, milk, and 1 tablespoon salad oil until smooth.

4. Gradually add flour mixture, beating until smooth. Then gently fold egg white into this batter.

5. Meanwhile, in deep skillet or deep-fat fryer, slowly heat salad oil or shortening (at least 2 inches) to 375°F. on deep-frying thermometer.

6. Drain sausages very well on paper towels; halve crosswise. Dip into batter, coating evenly.

7. Deep-fry a few at a time, turning once, 3 to 4 minutes, or until golden brown on both sides. Drain on paper towels.

8. Serve on wooden picks, with sharp mustard.

Makes about 42 fritters.

SWISS FONDUE

1 clove garlic, split	¾ cup dry white wine
1 pound natural Swiss cheese, grated	1 tablespoon cornstarch
½ teaspoon salt	2 tablespoons kirsch
Dash pepper	1 loaf French bread, cut into 1-inch cubes

1. Rub sides and bottom of a 2½-quart earthenware or flameproof casserole with garlic. Do not use a metal casserole.

2. Combine cheese, salt, pepper, and wine in casserole; cook, stirring, over medium heat, just until cheese melts.

3. Combine cornstarch and kirsch. Stir into cheese mixture; cook, stirring, 1 to 2 minutes, or until the mixture is smooth.

4. To serve: Set Fondue over candle warmer or a chafing-dish flame. Each bread cube is speared with fork and dipped into cheese mixture.

Makes 4 to 6 servings.

Note: If mixture thickens on standing, stir in a little more wine.

WARM PÂTÉ TART

2 (9-inch size) unbaked pie shells	4 cloves garlic, crushed
5 eggs	½ cup packaged dry bread crumbs
6 cans (4¾-ounce size) liver pâté	Nutmeg
¾ cup chopped onion	2 tablespoons butter or margarine

2 cups heavy cream
½ teaspoon salt
Dash cayenne

⅔ cup grated Parmesan cheese
¼ cup dry sherry

1. Prepare pie shells. Refrigerate.

2. Separate 1 egg, placing white in small bowl, yolk in large bowl. Beat egg white. Brush over pie shells.

3. Preheat oven to 375°F. In large bowl, combine pâté, ½ cup onion, the garlic, bread crumbs, and ½ teaspoon nutmeg; mix well. Spoon into prepared pie shells, spreading evenly.

4. In hot butter in small skillet, sauté remaining ¼ cup onion about 2 minutes, or until lightly golden. Set aside.

5. Add remaining 4 eggs to egg yolk. Beat with cream, salt, cayenne, and dash nutmeg until well combined but not frothy. Stir in sautéed onion, the cheese, and sherry. Pour half over pâté in each pie shell.

6. Bake 35 to 40 minutes, or until a knife inserted 1 inch from edge comes out clean.

7. Let cool on wire rack about 1 hour. Serve warm, each cut into 12 wedges.

Makes 24 servings.

QUICHE TARTLETS

Pastry

2½ cups sifted all-purpose flour
1½ teaspoons salt
1 cup shortening

6 to 8 tablespoons ice water
1 egg yolk, beaten

Filling

16 slices bacon, *or* 1 cup sliced
       stuffed green olives, *or* 6
       medium-size onions, sliced

1½ cups (6 ounces) grated
       natural Swiss cheese

4 eggs
2 cups light cream
¾ teaspoon salt
Dash nutmeg
Dash cayenne
Dash pepper

1. Make Pastry: Sift flour and salt into a bowl. Using pastry blender or two knives, cut half of shortening into flour mixture until mixture looks like coarse cornmeal.

2. Cut in remaining shortening until fat is the size of large peas.

3. Sprinkle ice water (1 tablespoon at a time) over different parts of flour mixture, mixing quickly, with a fork, after each addition; blend just until mixture holds together.

4. Turn out on waxed paper, and press into a ball.

5. Roll out one fourth dough at a time. Carefully fit pastry into tartlet pans.

6. Combine beaten egg yolk and 2 tablespoons water. Before filling tartlet shells, brush with this mixture, to prevent a soggy crust. Preheat oven to 400°F.

7. Prepare desired filling, and fill tartlet shells.

8. Into each tartlet, sprinkle 1 heaping teaspoon grated cheese.

9. Then beat eggs. Beat in light cream, salt, nutmeg, cayenne, and pepper. Pour 1 to 1½ tablespoons of this mixture over cheese in each tartlet.

10. Bake at 400°F. for 8 minutes; reduce heat to 350°F.; bake 5 to 8 minutes longer, or until filling puffs up and is golden brown. Serve hot.

Makes 43 tartlets, each 2½ to 3 inches wide and ½ inch deep.

Note: These can be baked early in the day. Do not brown completely, however. At serving time, brown at 400°F. for 3 to 5 minutes. Serve hot.

FILLING FOR BACON QUICHE

1. Fry bacon until crisp. Drain on paper towels, and crumble into bits.

2. Put 1 teaspoon of crumbled bacon in each pastry-lined tartlet pan.

FILLING FOR OLIVE QUICHE

1. Put a few olive slices into each pastry-lined pan.

FILLING FOR ONION QUICHE

1. Sauté sliced onions in 2 tablespoons butter or margarine until golden; drain.
2. In each pastry-lined tartlet pan, put about 1 teaspoon onions.

BLINIS

½ pound smoked salmon
2 cups packaged buckwheat-pancake mix
2½ cups milk
2 eggs
1¼ cups butter or margarine, melted

1 cup sour cream
1 jar (2 ounces) black beluga caviar

1. Cut salmon in paper-thin slices. Set aside.
2. In medium-size bowl, combine pancake mix, milk, eggs, and ½ cup butter.
3. With rotary beater, beat until batter is smooth.
4. Meanwhile, heat a 10-inch heavy skillet over low heat. To test temperature, drop a little water onto hot skillet; water should roll off in drops.
5. For each blini, coat pan with 1 teaspoon of the remaining melted butter. Pour in about ½ cup batter, tilting the skillet to spread batter over bottom.
6. Cook over medium heat until lightly browned on one side; turn, and brown other side. Remove to platter.
7. Place 2 or 3 slices salmon on half of blini; roll up. Place seam side down. Keep warm while making rest of blinis.
8. To serve: Place 2 blinis on a heated serving plate. Top each serving with about 2 tablespoons of remaining melted butter. Pass sour cream and caviar.

Makes 8 blinis; 4 servings.

BLINTZES

Cheese, Blueberry, Cherry, or
   Apple Filling (see pp. 94–95)

Blintzes

2   eggs
2   tablespoons salad oil
1   cup milk
¾   cup sifted all-purpose flour
½   teaspoon salt

About ¼ cup butter or margarine

Confectioners' sugar
1   cup dairy sour cream

1. Make one of Fillings.
2. Make Blintzes: In medium-size bowl, beat eggs, salad oil, and milk until well mixed. Add flour and salt; beat until smooth.
3. Refrigerate, covered, 30 minutes. Batter should be consistency of heavy cream.
4. For each blintz: Melt ½ teaspoon butter in a 10-inch skillet. Pour in 3 tablespoons batter, rotating pan quickly, to spread batter evenly. Cook over medium heat until lightly browned on underside; then remove from pan. Stack blintzes, browned side up, as you take them from skillet.
5. Place about 3 tablespoons of filling on browned surface of each blintz. Fold two opposite sides over filling; then overlap ends, covering filling completely.
6. Melt rest of butter in large skillet. Add 3 or 4 blintzes, seam side down; sauté until golden brown on underside; turn, and sauté other side. Keep blintzes warm in a low oven while cooking rest.
7. Sprinkle with confectioners' sugar. Serve hot, with sour cream. Makes 10.

CHEESE FILLING

1   package (3 ounces) cream
     cheese, softened
2   cups (1 pound) dry cottage
     cheese or ricotta cheese

1   egg yolk
2   tablespoons sugar
½   teaspoon vanilla extract

1. In medium-size bowl, combine cheeses, egg yolk, sugar, and vanilla; beat with electric mixer until smooth.
2. Refrigerate, covered, until ready to use.
Makes about 2½ cups.

BLUEBERRY FILLING

1   **can (1 pound, 4 ounces)**   ⅛ **teaspoon nutmeg**
     blueberry-pie filling

1. Combine pie filling and nutmeg in small bowl. Mix well.
Makes 2 cups.

CHERRY FILLING

1   **can (1 pound, 4 ounces)**   ⅛ **teaspoon cinnamon**
     cherry-pie filling

1. Combine pie filling and cinnamon in small bowl; mix well.
Makes 2 cups.

APPLE FILLING

2 **pounds tart cooking apples,**   1 **teaspoon cinnamon**
    pared, cored, and sliced   ⅛ **teaspoon nutmeg**
1 **cup sugar**

1. In medium-size saucepan, combine apples, sugar, cinnamon, and nutmeg. Cook over low heat, stirring occasionally, 15 minutes, or until apples are very tender.
2. Let cool, covered, about ½ hour.
Makes 2 cups.

CURRIED-CHICKEN CRÊPES

Chicken Filling

5 tablespoons butter or margarine
¼ cup all-purpose flour
Salt
1½ cups milk
1 teaspoon chopped shallot or green onion
2 cups cooked chicken or turkey in ¼-inch cubes

½ cup dry white wine
1 teaspoon curry powder
¼ teaspoon Worcestershire sauce
⅛ teaspoon pepper
Dash cayenne

Crêpes

1 cup milk
¾ cup unsifted all-purpose flour
¼ teaspoon salt

2 eggs

Salad oil

Topping

1 egg yolk
⅛ teaspoon salt
4 tablespoons butter or margarine, melted

2 teaspoons lemon juice
¼ cup heavy cream, whipped

Grated Parmesan cheese

1. Make Chicken Filling: To make white sauce, melt 4 tablespoons butter in medium-size saucepan; remove from heat. Stir in ¼ cup flour and ½ teaspoon salt until smooth. Gradually stir in milk; bring to boil, stirring constantly. Reduce heat, and simmer 5 minutes. Remove from heat, and set aside.

2. In 1 tablespoon hot butter in medium-size skillet, sauté shallot 1 minute. Add chicken; sauté 2 minutes longer. Add wine, curry, ¼ teaspoon salt, the Worcestershire, pepper, and cayenne; cook over medium heat, stirring, 3 minutes. Stir in 1 cup of the white sauce just until blended. Refrigerate while making crêpes. Set aside remaining white sauce for topping.

3. Make Crêpes: In medium-size bowl, with rotary beater, beat milk with flour and salt until smooth. Add eggs; beat until well combined.

4. Slowly heat a 5½-inch skillet until a little water sizzles when dropped on it. Brush pan lightly with salad oil. Pour about 1½ tablespoons batter into skillet, tilting pan so batter covers bottom.

5. Cook until nicely browned on underside. Loosen edge; turn; cook until browned on other side. Remove from pan; cool on wire rack. Then stack on waxed paper. Repeat with rest of batter, to make 18 crêpes. Lightly brush pan with oil before cooking each one.

6. Preheat oven to 350°F. Remove filling from refrigerator. Spoon 1 rounded tablespoon onto each crêpe; fold two opposite sides over filling. Arrange in shallow baking dish, seam side up; cover with foil. Bake 20 to 25 minutes, or until heated through.

7. Meanwhile, make Topping: In small bowl, with rotary beater, beat egg yolk with salt until foamy. Gradually beat in 2 tablespoons melted butter. Mix remaining butter with lemon juice; gradually beat into egg-yolk mixture. With wire whisk or rubber scraper, fold in remaining white sauce just until combined. Fold in whipped cream.

8. Uncover hot crêpes. Spoon topping over them; sprinkle lightly with grated Parmesan cheese. Broil, 4 to 6 inches from heat, until nicely browned. If desired, carefully transfer to chafing dish.

Makes 8 servings.

To prepare ahead of time: Make and fill crêpes as directed. Cover with foil and refrigerate. Make topping, but do not add whipped cream. Refrigerate. To serve: Bake crêpes as directed. Fold the whipped cream into topping; spoon over the crêpes. Sprinkle with cheese; broil as directed.

CRÊPES WITH CURRIED CRAB MEAT

Crab-Meat Filling

5 tablespoons butter or margarine
¼ cup all-purpose flour
Salt
1½ cups milk
1 can (7½ ounces) king-crab meat, drained

1 teaspoon chopped shallot or green onion
½ cup dry white wine
1 teaspoon curry powder
¼ teaspoon Worcestershire sauce
⅛ teaspoon pepper
Dash cayenne

Crêpes
   2 eggs
   1 cup milk
   ¾ cup sifted all-purpose flour

   ¼ teaspoon salt

   Salad oil

Glaze
   1 egg yolk
   ⅛ teaspoon salt
   4 tablespoons butter or
        margarine, melted

   2 teaspoons lemon juice
   ¼ cup heavy cream, whipped

   Grated Parmesan cheese

1. Make Crab-Meat Filling: For white sauce, melt 4 tablespoons butter in medium-size saucepan. Remove from heat. Add ¼ cup flour and ½ teaspoon salt; stir until smooth. Gradually stir in 1½ cups milk; bring to boil, stirring constantly. Reduce heat; simmer 5 minutes. Remove from heat, and set aside.

2. Separate crab-meat pieces, removing membrane. In 1 tablespoon hot butter in medium-size skillet, sauté shallot 1 minute. Add crab meat; sauté 2 minutes longer. Add wine, curry, ¼ teaspoon salt, the Worcestershire, pepper, and cayenne; cook over medium heat, stirring, 3 minutes. Stir in 1 cup of the white sauce just until blended. Turn into a bowl; refrigerate while making crêpes.

3. Make Crêpes: In medium-size bowl, combine 2 eggs, the milk, flour, and ¼ teaspoon salt; beat with electric mixer until smooth.

4. Slowly heat a 5½-inch skillet until a little water sizzles when dropped on it. Brush pan lightly with salad oil. Pour in 1½ tablespoons batter, rotating pan quickly, to spread batter over bottom of pan.

5. Cook over medium heat until nicely browned on underside; turn; cook until browned on other side. Remove from pan; cool on wire rack; stack on waxed paper. Repeat with rest of batter, to make 18 crêpes. Brush pan with oil before making each one.

6. Preheat oven to 350°F. Remove filling from refrigerator. Spoon 1 rounded tablespoon onto each crêpe; fold two opposite sides over filling. Arrange in shallow baking dish; cover with foil. Bake 20 to 25 minutes, or until heated through.

7. Meanwhile, make Glaze: In small bowl, with rotary beater, beat egg yolk with salt until foamy; gradually beat in 2 tablespoons melted butter. Mix remaining butter with lemon juice; gradually beat into egg-yolk mixture. With wire whisk or a rubber scraper, fold in the remaining white sauce just until it is combined. Fold in the whipped cream.

8. Uncover hot crêpes. Spoon glaze over them; then sprinkle lightly with Parmesan. Broil, 4 to 6 inches from heat, until nicely browned.

Makes 6 servings.

To prepare ahead of time: Make and fill crêpes as directed. Cover with foil, and refrigerate. Make glaze, but do not add whipped cream. Refrigerate. To serve: Bake crêpes as directed. Fold the whipped cream into glaze, ready to spoon over crêpes. Sprinkle with cheese.

CRÊPES WITH STRAWBERRIES AND SOUR CREAM

Crêpes

2 eggs	1½ cups sliced strawberries
½ cup milk	2 tablespoons granulated sugar
¼ cup flour	Confectioners' sugar
1 teaspoon salad oil	Dairy sour cream
Dash salt	
About 3 teaspoons butter or margarine	

1. Make Crêpes: In medium-size bowl, combine eggs, milk, flour, salad oil, and salt. Beat with electric mixer until smooth.

2. For each crêpe, melt ¼ teaspoon butter in 7-inch skillet. Pour in about 2 tablespoons batter, rotating pan quickly, to spread batter completely over bottom of pan.

3. Cook over medium heat until lightly browned on underside; turn, and brown other side. Make rest of crêpes (about 10). Stack crêpes in baking pan as they are removed from skillet. Keep warm in low oven.

4. Combine strawberries and granulated sugar. Place 2 tablespoons in center of each crêpe. Roll up, and sprinkle with confectioners' sugar. Serve immediately, with sour cream.

Makes 5 servings.

5

MEATS AND POULTRY

Meat or poultry is an essential part of every brunch menu, as a course in itself or as a filling for pancakes or a soufflé. The range of meats appropriate for brunch is unlimited, although kebabs, creamed poultry dishes, grilled or broiled chops, and whole buffet meats—such as glazed hams—are the most popular. Again, the primary consideration in choosing a meat is whether it will complement the other dishes on your menu.

Any glazed meat—buffet ham, corned beef, Canadian bacon, or tongue—is always a wise choice. Glazing enhances the flavor of meat. Whole meats are very attractive to serve; they require almost no preparation time and need only an occasional glance at the meat thermometer once they have been put in the oven. Serving is also quite simple: merely cut off a few slices, arrange them attractively on the platter, and allow each guest to help himself.

You may wish to grill or broil your main course instead of roasting it. Cut the meat into cubes and arrange them on skewers with pieces of tomato, onion, pepper, pineapple, mushroom, and bacon to fashion kebabs. Brush them with oil or butter and soy sauce if you wish, and grill six inches from the hot coals or three to four inches from a broiler flame. If whole onions are to be used, choose small ones and parboil them first by placing them in a large pot of boiling water for about fifteen minutes. Then add them to the skewers. Thick slices of onion may also be used. Kebabs are traditionally served on beds of rice, although they are equally good eaten alone and make a wonderful selection for an informal outdoor barbecue. Chunks of tender beef or lamb or chicken livers are the most popular choices for kebabs.

Grilled steaks, lamb and pork chops, and spareribs are all well worth preparing on your grill. Choose cuts that are not too thick—between one and two inches—and be sure that they are lightly streaked with fat. Trim away excess fat. Heat the rack over the coals, oil it to prevent sticking, and sear the meat well so that it will hold its juices. After searing, raise the grill several inches and cook, turning infrequently, until the meat is done to your liking. Because grill fires vary greatly in intensity and meat cuts vary so much in size and thickness, no exact timetable can be given.

Simple broiled steaks, prepared to just the right degree of doneness for each person's taste and seasoned with a dash of salt and freshly ground black pepper, can make a satisfying main dish for a brunch. Serve one large steak on a platter surrounded by scrambled eggs and grilled tomatoes or prepare individual servings accompanied by a fruit or vegetable salad. Below is a timetable which will produce steaks done exactly to your liking.

Timetable for Broiling Steaks

(For steaks at room temperature in preheated broiler)

Broil 1-inch-thick steaks (flank steak, ¾ inch) 3 inches from heat.
Broil 1½-inch-thick steaks (flank steak, 1 inch) 4 inches from heat.

Cut	Thickness	Approximate Minutes per Side		
		Rare	Medium	Well Done
Filet	1 inch	3 min	5 min	6-7 min
	1½ inches	8 min	9 min	11 min
Porterhouse	1 inch	6 min	8 min	11 min
	1½ inches	8 min	10 min	14 min
T-bone	1 inch	6 min	8 min	11 min
	1½ inches	9-10 min	11-12 min	14-15 min
Rib	1 inch	5-6 min	7 min	8-9 min
	1½ inches	9-10 min	11-12 min	14-15 min
Club	1 inch	5-6 min	7 min	8-9 min
	1½ inches	9 min	11 min	14-15 min

Cut	Thickness	Approximate Minutes per Side		
		Rare	Medium	Well Done
Delmonico	1 inch	5 min	7 min	8-9 min
	1½ inches	9 min	11-12 min	14-15 min
Shell or strip	1 inch	5 min	7 min	8-9 min
	1½ inches	9 min	10-11 min	14-15 min
Sirloin	1 inch	8-9 min	10 min	12 min
	1½ inches	12-14 min	14-15 min	17-18 min
Sirloin butt*	1 inch	4 min	6 min	
	1½ inches	12 min	14 min	
Sirloin tip*	1 inch	10 min	11-12 min	
	1½ inches	12 min	14 min	
Flank*	¾ inch	2 min	3 min	
	1 inch	3 min	4 min	
Butterfly* (eye of round)	1 inch	4 min	6 min	
	1½ inches	8-9 min	10 min	
Ground sirloin, round, or chuck patties	¾ inch	4 min	6 min	7 min

For easy service and an entertaining meal for all, try a beef fondue bourguignonne. All you need is a fondue pot, or an electric skillet, containing about a cup of oil—peanut oil works well—and about a half pound of one-inch raw beef cubes per person. Place a square of bread in the heated oil to prevent it from spattering. Each person will need a fondue fork and a choice of sauces—curried, sweet-sour, mustard- or mayonnaise-based mixed with herbs, or Sauce Robert (available commercially). Serve your fondue with French or Italian bread, a chilled soup, a tossed salad, and fresh fruit for dessert. To make certain that no one will accidentally burn his lips, provide your guests with dinner forks to which they can transfer the meat from the hot fondue forks.

Poultry is often a good choice for brunch because it is light, low in calories, versatile, and inexpensive. For a change from the usual chicken and turkey, try the recipe for Squab Chickens à la Grecque, stuffed with a delicate bread-crumb dressing.

*Use instant meat tenderizer as label directs.

If you decide to serve poultry, be sure to select a bird that is full-fleshed and moist-skinned, with pale skin and yellow fat. If you simply wish to roast the poultry, place the bird, trussed if it has been stuffed, breast side up on an oiled rack in a large shallow pan. Rub shortening into the breast and cover it lightly with cheesecloth or aluminum foil. Keep the cloth moist with pan drippings. Remove the cloth or foil for the last half hour of cooking time so that the bird will brown. Place the bird in a preheated 450°F. oven, reduce the temperature immediately to 350°F., and baste frequently. Allow approximately twenty minutes per pound roasting time. When the leg joint can be moved easily, the bird is done. Remove it from the oven and allow it to "rest" for fifteen or twenty minutes to facilitate carving.

Leftover meat and poultry may be cut up and added to omelets and soufflés or they may be creamed or curried and served in pastry shells or over rice. These dishes, in fact, are the ones traditionally associated with brunch. They are nourishing yet light in flavor and texture; they need few accompaniments—a salad or fruit compote is all that is necessary. To reduce preparation time for your brunch, buy patty shells or frozen pastry. To add color and create an attractive plate, garnish your creamed meat or poultry with fresh parsley, watercress, or sliced, blanched almonds.

MEATS

GRILLED BANANAS AND CANADIAN BACON

¾ cup butter-flavored syrup
2 tablespoons lemon juice
2 large ripe bananas

¾ pound Canadian bacon, sliced
2 tablespoons butter or
margarine

1. Combine syrup and lemon juice in shallow baking dish.
2. Peel bananas; halve lengthwise, then crosswise. Place bananas and bacon slices in syrup mixture, coating well.
3. Meanwhile, preheat griddle as manufacturer directs. Rub griddle with butter. Grill bananas and bacon about 5 minutes on each side, or until bananas are golden.
Makes 4 servings.

GLAZED CANADIAN BACON

1 (2½-pound) piece Canadian bacon, unsliced
Whole cloves

⅓ cup apricot jam
⅓ cup orange marmalade

2 teaspoons lemon juice
1½ tablespoons prepared mustard

1 unpeeled navel orange, sliced ⅛ inch thick

1. Preheat oven to 350°F.
2. With sharp knife, score top and side of bacon to make a diamond pattern, making cuts ⅛ inch deep and 1½ inches apart.
3. Insert a clove in center of each diamond.
4. In small saucepan, combine jam, marmalade, lemon juice, and mustard; heat slightly.
5. Spread glaze over entire top and side of bacon. Place on rack in roasting pan.
6. Bake, uncovered, 1¼ hours. Remove to serving platter. Garnish with halved orange slices. Slice bacon thinly.
Makes 8 servings.

HOMINY AND BACON

1 cup white hominy grits
1 teaspoon salt
3 beef-bouillon cubes
½ pound sliced bacon
⅓ cup chopped onion

½ cup coarsely chopped green pepper
1 can (1 pound) stewed tomatoes
⅛ teaspoon dried thyme leaves

1. Preheat oven to 350°F. Lightly grease a 2-quart casserole.
2. In large saucepan, bring 5 cups water to boil. Stir in hominy and salt; add bouillon cubes.
3. Over medium heat, cook, stirring occasionally, 40 minutes, or until very thick.
4. Meanwhile, in large skillet, slowly sauté bacon until almost crisp. Drain, reserving 2 tablespoons drippings.
5. In reserved drippings in skillet, sauté onion and green pepper about 5 minutes, or until tender.

6. Add tomatoes and thyme. Bring to boil; reduce heat, and simmer, uncovered, 10 to 12 minutes, or until slightly thickened.

7. Spread half of cooked hominy in bottom of prepared casserole; cover with tomato mixture, then with rest of hominy. Arrange bacon slices over top, to form a lattice.

8. Then bake, uncovered, for 30 minutes, or until the bacon is crisp and brown.

Makes 6 servings.

MUSTARD-FRUIT-GLAZED HAM

1 (10- to 12-pound) fully cooked, bone-in ham
1 cup light-brown sugar, firmly packed
¾ cup light corn syrup
⅓ cup prepared brown mustard
1 can (1 pound, 4½ ounces) sliced pineapple, drained

1 can (1 pound, 1 ounce) pear halves, drained
8 to 10 preserved kumquats, drained
8 to 10 maraschino cherries
1 small lime, thinly sliced

1. Preheat oven to 325°F. Place ham, fat side up, on rack in roasting pan. Insert meat thermometer in thickest part of ham, away from bone.

2. Bake, uncovered, 2½ hours.

3. Meanwhile, combine brown sugar, syrup, and mustard. Cook over low heat, stirring occasionally, until sugar is dissolved and mixture comes to boil.

4. In medium-size bowl, combine fruit with mustard mixture. Let stand at room temperature, basting the fruit several times, about 2 hours.

5. Remove any skin from ham; then score fat into 1-inch diamonds. Brush about ¼ cup syrup from fruit over ham; bake 15 minutes. Arrange pineapple slices, pears, kumquats, and cherries on ham; secure with wooden picks. Brush ham with about ¼ cup more syrup; bake 15 minutes, or until nicely glazed and meat thermometer registers 130°F. Place a slice of lime, curled up, in center of each pineapple slice. Pass remaining mustard fruit.

Makes 16 to 18 servings.

MEATS AND POULTRY

Timetable for Baking Fully Cooked Ham

Oven temperature—325°F.
Internal temperature—130°F.
on meat thermometer

Type of Ham	Weight (Pounds)	Approximate Baking Time (Hours)
Bone-in whole ham	14 to 18	3 to 3½
Bone-in whole ham	8 to 12	2¼ to 2¾
Bone-in half ham	6 to 8	2 to 2¼
Boneless whole ham	8 to 10	2½ to 3
Boneless quarter or half ham	2½ to 5	1½ to 1¾

BAKED HAM, SAUSAGE, AND BACON

1 (3-pound) canned ham
Whole cloves
2 tablespoons red-currant jelly
1 pound link sausage

1 pound sliced bacon

Pancakes (optional)

1. Preheat oven to 350°F. Place ham in shallow pan. Score with a sharp knife; stud with cloves. Melt jelly; spoon over ham.
2. Bake 30 minutes, or until heated.
3. Meanwhile, sauté sausage; cook bacon until crisp.
4. Serve with pancakes, if desired.
Makes 12 servings.

SAUTÉED APPLES AND SAUSAGES

1 package (8 ounces)
brown-and-serve sausages
1 can (1 pound, 4 ounces)
sliced apples, packed in syrup
1 can (5½ ounces) apricot
nectar

½ cup light corn syrup
⅛ teaspoon nutmeg

8 frozen packaged waffles
Butter or margarine

1. In large skillet, sauté sausages until nicely browned all over. Drain off fat.
2. Add undrained apples, apricot nectar, corn syrup, and nutmeg; bring to boil. Reduce heat, and simmer, stirring occasionally, until liquid is thickened.
3. Toast waffles. Spread each with butter.
4. Spoon apples and sausages over waffles.
Makes 4 servings.

HAM, PINEAPPLE, AND SAUSAGE KEBABS

1 (¾-pound) fully cooked ham
2 cans (4-ounce size) Vienna
sausage, drained

1 can (12 ounces) pineapple
chunks, drained
2 tablespoons butter or
margarine, melted

1. Cut ham into 24 chunks. On 6 or 8 wooden skewers, thread ham chunks alternately with sausages and pineapple. Arrange on rack of broiler pan.
2. Broil, 3 inches from heat, 10 minutes on a side, brushing with melted butter occasionally.
Makes 4 to 6 servings.

CREAMED CHIPPED BEEF OVER
TOASTED ENGLISH MUFFINS

2   cups boiling water
1   jar (5 ounces) sliced dried
    beef, chopped
2   tablespoons butter or
    margarine
1   package (1 ounce)
    white-sauce mix

½   teaspoon seasoned salt
1   cup milk

2   English muffins, split and
    toasted

1. In medium-size bowl, pour boiling water over dried beef; let stand several minutes. Drain beef well.

2. Melt butter in medium-size skillet. Add beef; sauté, stirring, several minutes.

3. Stir in white-sauce mix and seasoned salt; mix well. Gradually stir in milk.

4. Bring to boil, stirring. Reduce heat, and simmer until mixture is thickened.

5. Spoon over toasted English-muffin halves.

Makes 4 servings.

GLAZED CORNED BEEF

1   (8-pound) corned-beef brisket
2   medium-size onions,
    quartered
2   bay leaves

1   teaspoon salt
10 whole black peppers
1   clove garlic
4   whole cloves

Glaze
½   cup dark corn syrup

1   tablespoon prepared mustard

1. Put brisket in large kettle; cover with cold water.

2. Add onions, bay leaves, salt, black peppers, garlic, and cloves; bring to boil.

3. Reduce heat; simmer, covered, about 4 hours, or just until corned beef is fork-tender.

4. Remove corned beef from cooking liquid. Cool completely; refrigerate, covered, overnight.

5. Next day, make Glaze: In small saucepan, combine corn syrup and mustard.

6. Bring to boil over medium heat, stirring constantly. Reduce heat, and simmer, uncovered, stirring occasionally, 10 minutes. Remove from heat; let cool.

7. Trim any excess fat from corned beef. Place meat on rack in broiler pan. Brush top and sides with some of the glaze.

8. Run under broiler, 5 or 6 inches from heat, 10 minutes; brush several times with remaining glaze.

9. Let corned beef cool; refrigerate until ready to serve.
Makes 12 servings.

ENGLISH MIXED GRILL

3 veal kidneys
1 tablespoon cider vinegar

1 teaspoon salt

Butter Sauce
½ cup butter or margarine
2 tablespoons lemon juice
2 tablespoons finely chopped
   parsley

1 teaspoon salt
⅛ teaspoon pepper

Crumb Topping
2 tablespoons butter or
   margarine, melted
⅓ cup soft bread crumbs
¼ teaspoon dried basil leaves
¼ teaspoon dried rosemary
   leaves

6 loin lamb chops, cut 1 inch
   thick (about 2½ pounds)
3 medium-size tomatoes, halved
6 rump steaks, cut ½ inch thick
   (about 2½ pounds)
Instant meat tenderizer

12 slices bacon
 6 link sausages (1 pound)

Watercress

1. Rinse kidneys. Place in medium-size saucepan with 3 cups water, the vinegar, and 1 teaspoon salt; bring to boil. Lower heat, and simmer, covered, 10 minutes; drain. Split lengthwise. Refrigerate, covered, until ready to use.

2. Make Butter Sauce: Melt butter in small saucepan. Add lemon juice, parsley, salt, and pepper. Set aside.

3. Make Crumb Topping: In small bowl, combine melted butter, bread crumbs, basil, and rosemary. Set aside.

4. Pan-fry bacon in large skillet. Drain, one slice at a time, and immediately roll up and fasten with wooden pick, to form curl.

5. Place sausage in large skillet. Cover with cold water; bring to boil over moderate heat. Drain; then sauté, turning occasionally, until nicely browned.

6. Meanwhile, arrange lamb chops on rack in broiler pan. Brush well with some of Butter Sauce. Broil 6 inches from heat, 12 minutes.

7. Turn chops. Arrange tomatoes, cut side up, on broiler rack. Brush chops and tomatoes with Butter Sauce. Broil 12 minutes longer.

8. Meanwhile, sprinkle steaks with meat tenderizer as package label directs. When sausages are brown, remove, and keep warm. Discard drippings in skillet. Heat skillet; add steaks, and cook over high heat 3 to 5 minutes. Brush with Butter Sauce; turn; brush again with sauce, and cook 3 to 5 minutes longer, or until done as desired. Keep warm.

9. Remove chops to serving platter.

10. Divide Crumb Topping evenly over tomatoes. Arrange kidneys, cut side up, on broiler rack. Brush with Butter Sauce, and broil tomatoes and kidneys 1 to 2 minutes longer, or just until crumbs are golden.

11. Arrange bacon, sausage, steaks, and tomatoes on platter with the chops and kidneys. Garnish with watercress.

Makes 6 very large servings.

SHISH KEBAB

Marinade

3 tablespoons chopped fresh mint leaves

1 teaspoon dried tarragon leaves

3 tablespoons cider vinegar
½ cup light-brown sugar, firmly packed
1 teaspoon dry mustard
1 teaspoon salt
½ cup salad oil
¼ cup lemon juice
1 teaspoon grated lemon peel

3½ pounds boned leg of lamb, cut into 1¼-inch cubes
6 medium-size onions, peeled and halved crosswise
6 bacon slices, halved
12 whole cloves
4 medium-size green tomatoes, quartered

1. Make Marinade: Combine all ingredients in small saucepan; bring to boil, stirring. Reduce heat; simmer, uncovered, 5 minutes. Let cool.

2. Pour cooled marinade over lamb in shallow dish; refrigerate, covered, overnight.

3. Next day, in small amount of boiling water in tightly covered saucepan, simmer onions 10 minutes; drain, and cool. Wrap a strip of bacon around each onion half; secure with a clove.

4. Remove lamb, reserving marinade.

5. On 8 to 10 long skewers, thread lamb alternately with tomatoes and onions.

6. Adjust grill 6 inches from prepared coals. Grill kebabs about 15 minutes, turning them occasionally and brushing frequently with the marinade.

Makes 8 to 10 servings.

Note: To cook indoors, broil kebabs, 4 inches from heat, about 15 minutes, turning occasionally and brushing frequently with the marinade.

SUMATRA LAMB CURRY

¼ cup salad oil
3 pounds boneless shoulder of lamb, cut into 1-inch cubes
1 clove garlic, crushed
1 cup chopped onion
1½ to 2 tablespoons curry powder

1 cup coarsely chopped pared tart apple
1 tablespoon flour
2 tablespoons catsup
2 cups diced pared eggplant (about ½ pound)

½ cup coarsely chopped celery
1½ teaspoons salt
¼ teaspoon pepper
¼ bay leaf

2 teaspoons grated lemon peel
2 tablespoons light-brown sugar

6 cups hot cooked white rice

Curry Accompaniments

Chopped green pepper
Chutney
Whole salted peanuts
Flaked coconut
Coconut chips
Sliced banana, dipped in lemon
     juice

Raisins
Preserved kumquats
Sliced green onions
Chopped unpared cucumber
Yogurt
Pineapple chunks

1. In 2 tablespoons hot oil in Dutch oven or 6-quart heavy saucepan, sauté half of lamb cubes, turning, until browned on all sides—about 20 minutes. Remove lamb as it browns. Heat rest of oil; brown remaining lamb.

2. Add garlic, chopped onion, curry powder, and apple; sauté, stirring occasionally, until onion is tender—about 5 minutes. Remove from heat. Stir in flour. Then add 2 cups water, mixing well.

3. Add lamb cubes, catsup, eggplant, celery, salt, pepper, bay leaf, and lemon peel; stir to mix well.

4. Bring to boil. Reduce heat, and simmer, covered, until lamb is tender and liquid is reduced—about 1½ hours.

5. Stir in brown sugar; mix well.

6. Serve with rice and some of the curry accompaniments.
Makes 6 servings.

BROILED LAMB GRILL

6 tablespoons butter or
    margarine
3 tablespoons grated Parmesan
    cheese
3 firm tomatoes

1½ teaspoons oregano
6 loin lamb chops (cut 1½
    inches thick)
¼ cup lemon juice, fresh,
    frozen, or canned

½ cup olive oil

1 teaspoon tarragon

1 can (1 pound) cling-peach halves

⅓ cup currant jelly, melted

⅓ cup peach syrup

¼ teaspoon cloves

Dash cinnamon

Parsley or watercress

1. Remove broiler rack, and preheat broiling compartment to broil, or 550°F.

2. Work butter until soft; then blend in Parmesan cheese.

3. Slice tomatoes in half; sprinkle with oregano, and spread cut side with Parmesan-cheese mixture. Arrange on cold broiler rack.

4. Have lamb chops at room temperature.

5. Mix lemon juice, olive oil, and tarragon. Brush part of mixture on chops, and arrange chops on broiler rack.

6. Place broiling pan 4 inches from heat (chops will be about 2 inches from heat). *For medium chops:* Broil 5 to 6 minutes on first side; then turn; baste with more lemon-juice mixture, and broil 4 to 5 minutes. *For well-done chops:* Broil 6 to 8 minutes on first side; then turn, basting as above, and broil 5 to 7 minutes.

7. When chops are turned, place peach halves, pit side up, on broiler rack. Brush generously with melted currant jelly and peach syrup, to which spices have been added.

8. Serve, garnished with parsley or watercress, on a heated platter. Heat any remaining lemon-juice mixture, and pour it over the lamb chops.

Makes 6 servings.

LONDON BROIL

1 flank steak (about 2 pounds)

1 tablespoon salad oil

2 teaspoons chopped parsley

1 clove garlic, crushed

1 teaspoon salt

1 teaspoon lemon juice

⅛ teaspoon pepper

Sautéed onions (optional)

Baked potatoes (optional)

1. Wipe steak with damp paper towels. Trim fat from steak.

2. In cup, combine salad oil, chopped parsley, crushed garlic, salt, lemon juice, and pepper. Brush half of the oil mixture over the top of the steak.

3. Place the steak, oiled side up, on lightly greased broiler pan. Broil, 4 inches from heat, 5 minutes. Turn steak; brush with remaining oil mixture, and broil 4 to 5 minutes longer. The steak will be rare, which is the only way London Broil should be served.

4. Remove steak to a board or platter.

5. To serve: Slice steak very thinly, on diagonal, across the grain. Top each portion with sautéed onions and serve with baked potatoes, if desired.

Makes 4 servings.

Note: In many areas, in self-service meat departments, a cut of beef labeled London Broil (round steak) is sold. To prepare: While steak is still moist after being wiped with damp paper towels, sprinkle it with unseasoned meat tenderizer, as label directs. Then proceed as above, but omit salt from the oil mixture. Since this cut of beef is thicker than flank steak, increase the broiling time 2 minutes for each side.

SHEPHERD'S PIE

1 package (2 envelopes) instant mashed potatoes
1 tablespoon grated onion
1 egg, slightly beaten
2 cups finely chopped cooked beef
3 tablespoons finely chopped parsley
½ cup finely chopped celery

1 can (6 ounces) mushroom stems and pieces, finely chopped
1½ teaspoons salt
¼ teaspoon pepper
⅓ cup hot milk or cream
2 tablespoons grated Parmesan cheese
2 tablespoons butter or margarine

1. Prepare mashed potatoes as package label directs, adding grated onion to hot water required for potatoes. Beat in egg.

2. In a bowl, mix beef, 2 tablespoons parsley, celery, mushrooms, salt, pepper, and hot milk or cream.

3. Preheat oven to 400°F. Lightly grease a 2-quart casserole.

4. Spoon half the potato mixture (about 2 cups) into bottom of casserole; cover with meat, and top evenly with remaining potatoes. Sprinkle with grated cheese and remaining 1 tablespoon parsley; dot with butter.

5. Bake, uncovered, 20 to 25 minutes, or until surface is golden brown.

Makes 6 servings.

STEAK-AND-KIDNEY PIE

2½ packages (9½- to 11-ounce size) piecrust mix

2 pounds chuck, cut into strips, 2 inches by 1 inch

¼ cup unsifted all-purpose flour

6 tablespoons butter or margarine

2 veal kidneys, thinly sliced

1 can (7 ounces) frozen oysters, thawed and drained

2 cans (10¾-ounce size) beef gravy

¼ pound fresh mushrooms, washed and halved

1 cup chopped onion

2 tablespoons chopped parsley

½ bay leaf

1 teaspoon dried thyme leaves

1 teaspoon salt

¼ teaspoon pepper

1. Prepare piecrust mix as package label directs; refrigerate until ready to use.

2. Roll chuck strips in flour to coat evenly.

3. In hot butter in large skillet, brown chuck well on all sides. Arrange around sides of a 13- by 9- by 2-inch baking dish.

4. Preheat oven to 350°F.

5. In large bowl, combine kidneys, oysters, gravy, mushrooms, onion, parsley, bay leaf, thyme, salt, and pepper; mix well. Turn into center of baking dish; set aside.

6. On lightly floured surface, roll one third of dough ¼ inch thick. Cut into strips 1 inch wide.

7. Place strips around inside top edge of baking dish. Dampen edges slightly with water.

8. Roll remaining pastry to a 14- by 10-inch rectangle. Place over pastry strips, sealing edges; press edges firmly with tines of fork.

9. In center of pie, cut out a small rectangle, 3 by 2 inches, to form an air vent.

10. Bake pie 1¾ to 2 hours, or until beef is tender.

Makes 8 servings.

SMOKED TONGUE WITH FRUIT SAUCE

1 (4-pound) smoked beef tongue
2 cans (1-pound size) stewed tomatoes
2 cans (8½-ounce size) crushed pineapple, drained
2 tablespoons lemon juice

1 cup orange juice
¼ teaspoon salt
⅛ teaspoon pepper
1 tablespoon cornstarch
1 can (1 pound, 14 ounces) large pear halves, drained

1. Place tongue in large kettle. Cover with cold water.

2. Bring to boil. Reduce heat, and simmer, covered, 2 hours.

3. Drain tongue; let cool slightly. Trim off fat and gristle at root end. With tip of paring knife, slit skin on underside from thick end to tip. Carefully peel off; discard.

4. In same kettle, combine tomatoes, pineapple, lemon juice, orange juice, salt, and pepper; mix well. Bring to boil. Reduce heat, and simmer, uncovered, 5 minutes.

5. Add tongue; simmer, covered, 1½ hours, or until tongue is fork-tender. Turn tongue several times during cooking.

6. Fifteen minutes before end of cooking time, add cornstarch combined with 1 tablespoon water. Cook 15 minutes longer, until sauce is slightly thickened. Add pears; heat through.

7. To serve: Slice tongue, and arrange down center of serving platter. Surround with sauce and pear halves.

Makes 6 servings.

SWEETBREADS IN WHITE WINE IN PATTY SHELLS

2 pounds sweetbreads
2½ teaspoons salt
Ice water
1 package (6 ounces) frozen patty shells
6 tablespoons butter or margarine
½ cup thinly sliced carrot
½ cup thinly sliced onion

6 medium-size mushrooms, halved
1 cup dry white wine
¼ cup flour
¾ cup light cream
⅓ cup condensed chicken broth, undiluted

Chopped parsley

1. Soak sweetbreads in cold water to cover 1 hour; drain.
2. Bring 2 quarts water to boil in large saucepan. Add sweetbreads and 2 teaspoons salt; return to boiling. Reduce heat, and simmer, covered, 20 minutes.
3. Drain sweetbreads. Plunge into ice water, to keep white and firm; let cool completely in the water. Remove outer membrane and any fat in folds of sweetbreads. Pat dry with paper towels. Cut into about 1-inch cubes. (You should have 3 cups sweetbreads.)
4. Bake patty shells as package label directs. Keep warm.
5. In 2 tablespoons butter in a skillet, sauté carrot and onion until soft—about 5 minutes. Add sweetbreads; cook over medium heat, stirring occasionally, about 20 minutes, or until lightly browned.
6. Meanwhile, in 2 tablespoons butter in large saucepan, sauté mushrooms until golden— about 5 minutes. Add to sweetbread mixture with ½ cup wine; simmer, covered, 5 minutes.
7. In same saucepan, melt remaining butter. Remove from heat; blend in flour and remaining ½ teaspoon salt. Gradually stir in cream and undiluted chicken broth; bring to boil, stirring constantly. Reduce heat, and simmer 1 minute.
8. Stir in sweetbread mixture and liquid and remaining wine; bring mixture just to boiling.
9. Spoon about ⅔ cup sweetbreads and sauce into and over each patty shell on individual serving plates. Cover with pastry tops; sprinkle with parsley.
Makes 6 servings.

POULTRY

CHICKEN LIVERS EN BROCHETTE

1½ pounds chicken livers (about 18)
¾ teaspoon dried marjoram leaves
¾ teaspoon dried thyme leaves
¾ teaspoon salt
⅛ teaspoon pepper
12 large fresh mushrooms
9 slices bacon, halved crosswise
6 tablespoons butter or margarine, melted
¼ cup dry white wine

1. Rinse chicken livers; pat dry with paper towels.
2. In medium-size bowl, combine the marjoram, thyme, salt, and pepper. Add livers; toss to combine.
3. Remove stems from mushrooms. Wipe mushroom caps with damp towels.
4. Wrap each liver in bacon. On each of 6 skewers, alternate 3 livers and 2 mushrooms. Arrange skewers on rack in broiling pan. Brush with half of butter.
5. Broil, 4 inches from heat, 5 minutes. Turn skewers; brush with remaining butter and the wine. Broil 5 to 7 minutes longer, or until bacon is crisp (livers should still be pink on inside).
Makes 6 servings.

CHICKEN LIVERS CHASSEUR

1 pound chicken livers
3 tablespoons butter or margarine
½ pound mushrooms, sliced
½ cup sliced onion
1 teaspoon flour
1 can (8 ounces) tomatoes
½ cup dry white wine
2 teaspoons chopped parsley
½ teaspoon salt
½ teaspoon Worcestershire sauce

Toast points
Chopped parsley (optional)

1. Wash chicken livers; drain on paper towels. Cut each in half.

2. In hot butter in large skillet, quickly brown chicken livers—about 5 minutes. Remove as browned.

3. Add mushrooms and onion to skillet; sauté until golden—about 5 minutes. Remove from heat.

4. Stir in flour, tomatoes, wine, parsley, salt, and Worcestershire; simmer, stirring frequently, about 5 minutes. Add chicken livers; simmer 5 minutes longer.

5. Turn into serving dish. Surround with toast points. Sprinkle with chopped parsley, if desired.

Makes 4 servings.

BREAST OF CHICKEN BENEDICT

3 whole chicken breasts (about 3 pounds)
1 medium-size onion, quartered
2 stalks celery with tops
2 sprigs parsley
1 teaspoon salt
3 whole black peppers
4 egg yolks

½ cup butter or margarine, melted
3 tablespoons lemon juice

Toast or toasted split English muffins, buttered
Marinated Asparagus (see p. 164)
Chopped parsley
Lemon wedges

1. Wash chicken breasts. Place in large saucepan with 1 quart water, the onion, celery, parsley, salt, and black peppers; bring to boil. Reduce heat, and simmer, covered, 40 minutes, or until chicken is tender.

2. Let stand, uncovered, 30 minutes; then refrigerate, covered, about 30 minutes, or until cool enough to handle. Remove chicken breasts from broth. Strain broth; set aside ½ cup. (Refrigerate remaining broth, to use as desired.)

3. Remove skin and bones from chicken breasts. Refrigerate, covered, until well chilled—at least 2 hours.

4. Meanwhile, bring reserved broth to boil.

5. In top of double boiler, with wire whisk or electric mixer, beat egg yolks well. Gradually beat in melted butter, then boiling broth.

6. Cook over hot, not boiling, water, stirring constantly, until mixture is thickened—about 5 minutes. Remove from hot water. Stir in lemon juice.

7. Refrigerate, covered, until sauce is chilled—about 2 hours.

8. To serve: Place chicken pieces on triangles of toast or English muffins. Arrange on platter alternately with bundles of Marinated Asparagus. Spoon sauce over chicken. Garnish with chopped parsley and lemon wedges.

Makes 6 servings.

CHICKEN CURRY

1 cup sliced onion	4 teaspoons curry powder
1 cup sliced carrots	2 tablespoons prepared chutney
2 teaspoons salt	2 tablespoons chopped
½ teaspoon pepper	crystallized ginger
1 chicken-bouillon cube,	1 tablespoon Worcestershire
crumbled	sauce
1 (4-pound) broiler-fryer, cut	¼ cup lime juice
up and skinned	
1 cup milk	1½ cups raw regular white rice
1 cup shredded coconut	¾ cup halved salted peanuts
1 tablespoon butter or	
margarine	¼ cup heavy cream
2 tablespoons flour	

1. Cover bottom of 4-quart Dutch oven, or large kettle, with onion and carrots. Sprinkle with salt and pepper.

2. Add bouillon cube and 1 cup water. Arrange chicken pieces over vegetables; bring mixture to boil. Reduce heat; simmer, covered, 1 hour, or until chicken is tender.

3. Meanwhile, in small saucepan, heat milk until bubbles form around edge of pan. Add coconut, mixing well. Cover, and set aside to cool.

4. Remove chicken; let cool. Then cut off meat in large pieces.

5. Drain vegetables, reserving broth. Set vegetables aside. Skim off any fat from broth. If necessary, add water to measure 2 cups broth.

6. Melt butter in same Dutch oven. Remove from heat. Stir in flour and curry powder until blended. Gradually add coconut-milk mixture and broth.

7. Bring to boil, stirring. Reduce heat; simmer, covered, 15 minutes.

8. Add chicken, reserved vegetables, chutney, ginger, Worcestershire, and lime juice; simmer, uncovered, 20 minutes, stirring occasionally.

9. Meanwhile, cook rice as label directs; drain, if necessary. Add peanuts, tossing lightly to combine.

10. Just before serving, stir cream into curry. Serve hot, over rice. Makes 6 servings.

CURRIED-CHICKEN-SALAD MOLD

2 envelopes unflavored gelatin
1 can (10½ ounces) condensed cream-of-chicken soup, undiluted
1 chicken-bouillon cube, dissolved in 1 cup boiling water
2 tablespoons lemon juice
1½ teaspoons curry powder

1 cup coarsely chopped cooked chicken
¼ cup chopped pimiento
¼ cup sweet-pickle relish, drained

4 pimiento-stuffed olives, sliced
Watercress sprigs

1. In large bowl, sprinkle gelatin over ½ cup cold water; let stand 5 minutes to soften.

2. In small saucepan, heat chicken soup with 1 cup water. Add gelatin, stirring until gelatin is dissolved.

3. Remove from heat. Stir in bouillon and lemon juice.

4. Blend curry powder with 1½ tablespoons cold water, stirring to dissolve curry powder. Stir into gelatin mixture.

5. Refrigerate until consistency of unbeaten egg white—about 1½ to 2 hours.

6. Fold in chicken, pimiento, and pickle relish. Turn into a 5-cup mold.

7. Refrigerate until firm—2 to 3 hours, or overnight.

8. To unmold: Run a small spatula around edge of mold. Invert over platter; shake to release. If necessary, place a hot, wet dishcloth over bottom of mold; shake to release.

9. To serve, garnish with sliced olives and watercress sprigs.

Makes 4 to 6 servings.

POACHED CHICKEN EN GELÉE

1 (5 to 5½-pound) ready-to-cook roasting chicken
2 stalks celery with tops, cut up
2 medium-size onions, peeled
2 whole cloves
1 large carrot, pared
6 whole black peppers
3 teaspoons salt
1 bay leaf
1 enveloped unflavored gelatin

1 cup canned madrilène
1 cup rosé wine
⅛ teaspoon liquid gravy seasoning
Watercress

Marinated Summer Vegetables (see p. 123)
Crisp lettuce leaves
Chopped parsley
Sauce Verte (see p. 124)

1. Rinse chicken, neck, and giblets (discard liver). Place chicken, breast side down, in 8-quart kettle. Add 1½ quarts water, the giblets, neck, celery, onions, each stuck with a clove, carrot, peppers, salt, and bay leaf.

2. Bring to boil over high heat. Reduce heat, and simmer, covered, 45 minutes. Carefully turn chicken with two wooden spoons; simmer, covered, 35 to 40 minutes longer, or until chicken is tender. Remove from heat.

3. Let stand, uncovered, 1 hour, frequently spooning broth over chicken. Carefully lift chicken and carrot to a baking pan; place chicken breast side up. Cover lightly with plastic film. Chill in refrigerator. Use broth another day.

4. To glaze chicken: Sprinkle gelatin over ½ cup madrilène in small saucepan, to soften. Place over low heat, stirring until gelatin is dissolved. Remove from heat.

5. Stir in remaining madrilène, the wine, and gravy seasoning. Set in a pan of ice and water. Let stand, stirring several times, until mixture is consistency of unbeaten egg white—about 10 minutes.

6. Arrange chilled chicken, breast side up, on rack set on tray. Spoon some of the gelatin mixture over chicken, coating completely.

7. Slice reserved carrot very thin. Dip, along with watercress, in gelatin mixture, and arrange on chicken breast, forming a V. Spoon remaining gelatin mixture over all, to coat evenly. If gelatin mixture becomes too stiff, place pan in warm water. Continue spooning on gelatin mixture that has run down onto tray—remelting it as necessary—until chicken is well glazed with a coating about ¼ inch thick.

8. Refrigerate until gelatin coating is firm—at least 1 hour.

9. To serve: Arrange chicken on serving platter, with Marinated Summer Vegetables and lettuce. Sprinkle vegetables with parsley. Pass Sauce Verte.

Makes 6 servings.

MARINATED SUMMER VEGETABLES

3 small yellow squash (1¼ pounds)
½ teaspoon salt
Bottled Italian-style dressing

1 teaspoon vinegar
1 large cucumber, thinly sliced
3 medium-size tomatoes, sliced

1. Wash squash. Cut on the diagonal into ¼-inch-thick slices. Cook in ½ cup water with the salt 12 to 15 minutes, or until squash is just tender, not mushy. Drain well.

2. Place squash in a shallow bowl. Add ½ cup dressing and the vinegar; toss gently, being careful not to break slices. Refrigerate, covered, until well chilled—about 2 hours.

3. Place cucumber and tomato slices in a shallow dish. Add ½ cup dressing. Refrigerate, covered, until chilled—at least 30 minutes.

Makes 6 servings.

SAUCE VERTE

1 cup mayonnaise or cooked salad dressing	2 tablespoons chopped parsley
2 tablespoons finely cut chives	2 tablespoons light cream
	1 tablespoon lemon juice

1. In small bowl, combine all ingredients; mix well.
2. Refrigerate, covered, until well chilled—at least 30 minutes.
Makes about 1 cup.

CHICKEN IN PATTY SHELLS

1 package (10 ounces) frozen patty shells	2 tablespoons butter or margarine
3 whole chicken breasts, boned and skinned (1½ pounds)	¼ cup dry sherry
1 can (10½ ounces) condensed cream-of-chicken soup, undiluted	¼ cup heavy cream
	½ cup salted peanuts or almonds
	2 tablespoons frozen chopped chives

1. Bake patty shells as package label directs.
2. Meanwhile, cut chicken breasts into 2-inch pieces.
3. Heat butter in Dutch oven. Add chicken; cook over medium heat, covered, stirring occasionally, 10 minutes.
4. Add cream-of-chicken soup, sherry, cream, salted peanuts, and chives; bring to boil, stirring. Lower heat, and simmer, uncovered, 5 minutes.
5. Serve in patty shells.
Makes 6 servings.

SQUAB CHICKENS À LA GRECQUE

3 onions	3 stalks celery
3 carrots	½ cup butter

Stuffing

½ cup chopped green onions
2 tablespoons butter
3 cups toasted bread crumbs
1 small clove garlic
2 tablespoons celery, finely chopped
1 tablespoon chopped parsley
½ cup pine nuts
1 teaspoon salt

Pinch pepper
Pinch rosemary
3 tablespoons cognac

6 squab chickens (or 1½-pound broilers)
1 cup chicken broth
3 cups hot cooked rice
½ cup white wine

1. Cut onions, carrots, celery into match-thick strips.

2. Melt butter in saucepan; add vegetables; cook, tossing them like a salad, about 5 minutes. Transfer to roasting pan.

3. Make the Stuffing: Cook chopped green onions in 2 tablespoons butter about 2 minutes.

4. Mix with remaining stuffing ingredients; fill cavities of birds; close openings with toothpicks or small skewers. Arrange birds on top of vegetables.

5. Bake in preheated 450°F. oven 20 minutes.

6. Add chicken broth. Baste frequently. Cover; reduce oven heat to 300°F.; roast 30 minutes more, or until legs of little birds feel tender when pinched.

7. To serve: Arrange drained vegetables and chickens on hot rice. Pour white wine into pan with broth; cook rapidly several minutes to reduce liquid slightly. Serve with birds.

Makes 6 servings.

VOL-AU-VENT WITH CHICKEN AND MUSHROOMS SUPREME

Pastry Shell

3 packages (14-ounce size) refrigerated turnover pastries (any flavor)
1 egg

Chicken and Mushrooms Supreme (see p. 127)

Watercress (optional)

1. Make Pastry Shell: Preheat oven to 400°F. Cut 2 circles from brown paper to fit 9-inch round layer-cake pan. In small bowl, lightly beat egg with ½ teaspoon water.

2. Unroll pastry from 2 packages turnover pastries (keep remaining package refrigerated until ready to use). To make base of shell: On floured board, fit 9 squares of pastry together to make a 9-inch square, pinching together perforations and edges. Place one paper circle on pastry as pattern; cut out pastry circle. Invert into a 9-inch layer-cake pan, paper side down.

3. For side of shell, cut remaining 7 pastry squares (still attached), lengthwise, into strips about 1 inch wide. Brush 1-inch-wide band around edge of pastry circle with some of beaten egg. Then fit strips of pastry to make a single layer around edge. Brush with beaten egg. Cover with a second layer of pastry strips. (Place second row of strips so that perforations in pastry do not cover perforations in bottom row.) Brush top with beaten egg.

4. Bake 20 minutes, or until deep golden brown. Let cool in pan on wire rack.

5. For second layer of side, place remaining paper circle in a 9-inch layer-cake pan.

6. Unroll remaining package of pastry; refrigerate 4 squares. Cut other 4 squares (still attached) into 1-inch-wide strips, as in step 3, and fit inside pan at outer edge to form a ring. Brush with beaten egg. Cover with a second layer of pastry strips, and brush with egg.

7. Bake 10 minutes, or until deep golden brown. Cool in pan on wire rack.

8. For "lid" of shell: On floured board, fit reserved 4 pastry squares together to make a 6-inch square, pinching together perforations and edges. From pastry square, cut a circle about 6 inches in diameter; with paring knife, lightly score top into diamonds. Brush with beaten egg.

9. Brush a scrap of pastry with beaten egg; cover with a second piece of pastry. Cut out a 1-inch diamond. Place on center top of lid; brush with beaten egg. Place lid on piece of brown paper; set on cookie sheet.

10. Bake 15 minutes, or until deep golden brown. Cool on cookie sheet on wire rack.

11. To serve: Remove brown paper from all pastry. Set shell on serving plate; carefully place ring on shell. Fill with Chicken and Mushrooms Supreme. Top with lid. Garnish with watercress, if desired. Makes 6 servings.

CHICKEN AND MUSHROOMS SUPREME

4 chicken breasts, boned (2½ to 3 pounds)
6 tablespoons butter or margarine
1 small onion, finely chopped
Salt
¼ teaspoon pepper

½ pound mushrooms, cut in thick slices
⅓ cup unsifted all-purpose flour
1½ cups heavy cream
¼ cup dry sherry
½ cup toasted blanched almonds

1. Remove skin from chicken breasts. Wipe chicken with damp paper towels. Then cut into 1-inch cubes.

2. In 2 tablespoons hot butter in Dutch oven, sauté onion until golden brown—about 5 minutes. Add chicken; sprinkle with 1 teaspoon salt and the pepper; add ½ cup water. Simmer, covered, 30 minutes, or until chicken is tender. Turn chicken occasionally. Add mushrooms; simmer, covered, 5 minutes longer.

3. Remove chicken and mushrooms from pan, and set aside. Pour liquid into a 1-cup measure (if necessary, add water to make 1 cup).

4. Melt remaining butter in the Dutch oven. Remove from heat. Stir in flour and ½ teaspoon salt until smooth. Gradually stir in the 1 cup liquid and the cream.

5. Bring to boil, stirring constantly. Reduce heat, and simmer 3 minutes. Add chicken and mushrooms and sherry; return to boiling. Reduce heat, and simmer, uncovered, 5 minutes.

6. Stir in almonds just before serving.

Makes 6 servings.

Note: The pastry shell and lid may be made and baked the day before or several hours before serving. At serving time, reheat on cookie sheet in 350°F. oven 5 minutes, or just until crisp and warm. Then assemble and fill, as above.

BREAST OF TURKEY CHAUD-FROID

1 (9- to 10-pound) frozen
ready-to-cook turkey breast,
thawed
Salt
Pepper
2 bay leaves, crumbled
1 medium onion, peeled and
sliced

3 envelopes unflavored gelatin
¾ cup mayonnaise or cooked
salad dressing
Ice water
2 cans (4¾-ounce size) liver
pâté

Decoration

1 white turnip, pared
1 carrot, pared

Chives

Watercress

1. Day before: Preheat oven to 325°F. Wipe thawed turkey with damp paper towels. Place on rack in roasting pan. Insert meat thermometer in thickest part.

2. Sprinkle with 1 tablespoon salt, ¼ teaspoon pepper, and bay leaves. Cover with onion slices. Cover pan with foil.

3. Roast 2½ to 3 hours, or until turkey is tender and meat thermometer registers 180°F., or as package label directs.

4. Remove turkey from pan, and strain broth. Cool turkey 1 hour. Refrigerate turkey and broth, covered, overnight.

5. Next day: Skim fat from broth. Heat broth in medium-size saucepan. Measure 2 cups. (If necessary, add canned chicken broth to make 2 cups.) Pour broth back into saucepan.

6. Sprinkle gelatin over ¾ cup cold water in small bowl; let stand 5 minutes, to soften. Add to hot broth, and heat, stirring, until gelatin is dissolved.

7. Place mayonnaise in medium-size bowl; beat with wire whisk or wooden spoon until creamy and smooth. Gradually add gelatin mixture, beating constantly. Set bowl in ice water; let stand, stirring occasionally, until chilled but not thickened—about 20 minutes.

8. Meanwhile, remove all skin from turkey. Place on wire rack set on a tray. Spread liver pâté over turkey, making sure surface is smooth. Remove mayonnaise mixture from ice, and carefully spoon over turkey, to cover completely.

9. Refrigerate until coating sets—about 30 minutes. Remove any coating on tray. Heat until melted; then set in ice water again to chill. Slowly spoon over turkey, coating completely. Refrigerate until set.

10. If there is still considerable coating on tray, reheat; chill, and spoon over turkey.

11. Meanwhile, prepare Decoration: At widest part of turnip, cut 2 crosswise slices ¼ inch thick. Using scalloped cookie cutters, cut one slice into a large flower and other slice into a medium-size flower.

12. Cut a ¼-inch-thick strip lengthwise from center of carrot. Using cookie cutters, cut into 2 or 3 small flowers.

13. When last coating on turkey is slightly chilled, gently press turnip and carrot flowers into coating, to decorate. Add chives for stems. Return to refrigerator until decoration is set.

14. To serve: Arrange turkey on platter. Let stand at room temperature about 30 minutes. Garnish with watercress.

Makes 10 to 12 servings.

BREAST OF TURKEY FLORENTINE
IN SCALLOP SHELLS

2 packages frozen chopped spinach
4 tablespoons butter
1 tablespoon Madeira
¼ cup flour
1½ cups turkey or chicken stock
⅓ cup heavy cream
Salt

Cayenne
3 tablespoons each grated Parmesan and Swiss cheese, combined
2 cups cooked breast of turkey, cut in 1½-inch dice
¼ cup dry bread crumbs
Butter

1. Cook the frozen spinach, covered, in 2 tablespoons of butter until thoroughly defrosted.

2. Uncover; raise the heat, and boil away the accumulated liquid.

3. Press the spinach in a sieve to remove any extra moisture; then purée it through a food mill (*not* a blender).

4. Add the Madeira, and put the spinach aside.

5. In a small pan, melt 2 tablespoons of butter, and add the flour. Mix to a paste, and pour in the stock.

6. Stirring with a whisk, bring the sauce to a boil, and cook until thick. Simmer for 5 minutes, and stir in the cream. Season with salt and a pinch of cayenne.

7. Mix 3 tablespoons of this sauce into the spinach purée. Then, to the remainder, add 4 tablespoons of the combined cheeses.

8. Butter 4 large scallop shells. Leaving a ½-inch border of each shell exposed, fill with the spinach, and arrange diced turkey on top.

9. Mask with the cheese sauce, and sprinkle each shell with a tablespoon of bread crumbs and then the remaining grated cheese.

10. Dot lightly with butter, and bake for about 15 minutes in a preheated 375°F. oven. When they begin to bubble, brown briefly under a broiler, and serve.

Makes 4 servings.

6

SEAFOOD

Until recently, only those Americans who lived in coastal states were able to enjoy fish all the time. With the advent of frozen foods, however, all types of seafood from lobster to New England cod have become readily available across the country. Seafood is now more popular than ever before, probably due to the increased emphasis on healthful eating. Fish is high in protein and iodine content and is low in cholesterol. It can be prepared with many variations to produce dishes that will please family and friends.

Fish has long been the staple food of the poor in almost every country of the world and was a mainstay of America's early colonists. The wealthy classes as well soon acquired a taste for fish, and seafood has had its place on elegant tables for the last two hundred years.

Because of the increasing pollution of our waters, seafood prices continue to rise, as fewer fish survive each year. Still, prices of fish are generally lower than those of meats. Your fish dealer can help you select fine quality seafood for any of the following recipes.

Fish and shellfish make wonderful brunch selections since they are light and versatile enough to complement other dishes. When selecting a fish, be sure it does not have a fishy odor. Check to see that the flesh of the fish is firm, that its eyes are bulging, its gills clean, and its skin shiny. One way to test for freshness is to place the fish in cold water. If it floats, it is fresh. If you buy frozen fish, make certain that it is still frozen when you purchase it; if it is not, do not refreeze it. The sooner you cook a fish after bringing it home from market, the more flavorful and nutritious it will be. No matter how you choose to prepare it—deep-fat-fried, sautéed, broiled, poached, pan-fried, or baked—if you do not overcook it, it will remain tender and delicate. The flavor will be even better if the fish is cooked with its skin on. In most of the following recipes, other types of fish may be substituted for those specified.

Shellfish also must be as fresh as possible for cooking. Oysters, of course, are in season only during the months containing an *r* in their names. To test these for freshness, and to test clams and mussels also, make certain that their shells are tightly clamped together. To clean them, scrub them under cold running water with a wire brush; then allow them to soak in several changes of cold water to which cornmeal or salt has been added. Shucking them will be easier if they are first placed on ice for a while. Fresh oyster meats are also available in supermarkets, packed with their own liquid in cardboard containers, and clams are often canned. When selecting scallops, choose only those that smell sweet, and remember that bay scallops are more tender than the larger white sea scallops. Both crabs and lobsters should be purchased and cooked while they are still alive and active. Shrimp should be dry and firm. Shell and devein them (toothpicks are useful for this) before eating. All shellfish should be cooked as soon as possible, although it will keep up to several days in the refrigerator. To retain its fine flavor, never overcook it.

Of course, it is also possible to entertain outdoors when you have decided on a seafood menu for your brunch. *Clambakes,* although usually held at the seashore, can make an unusual and refreshing back-yard or patio brunch. The pit method is perhaps the best known and most colorful way to prepare a clambake, but the kitchen range or outdoor grill offers a simpler, and in some ways more practical, alternative. No matter what method you decide to use, allow about one dozen steamer clams, one one-pound lobster, one quarter of a broiler-fryer chicken, one ear of corn, one baking potato, and one small onion for each person. Wrap the different foods in individual foil packets.

If you decide to prepare a pit, it should be dug in sand, although this is not essential. A hole four feet square and one foot deep will be sufficient to prepare food for from twenty to twenty-five persons. Line the pit with round rocks and build a hardwood fire on the rocks; keep the fire burning from two to three hours. When the rocks are thoroughly heated, remove the embers and cover the rocks with a six-inch layer of rock seaweed that has been soaked for at least forty-five minutes to remove sand and sediment. Wrapping each portion in cheesecloth will facilitate serving, but the food may also be packed into the pit in layers. If food is layered, seaweed may be placed between each layer. Use the hulls from the corn for the top layer (some of the hull should be left on each ear), sprinkle the food with seawater, and cover the pit quickly with a wet tarpaulin, weighting the edges of the tarp with rocks. Allow the food to steam for about an hour, or until the clams have opened. The tarp should puff up during the bake, indicating that the clams are getting plenty of steam.

If you lack the energy or wherewithal for a pit clambake, the range and grill methods are satisfactory substitutes. For either method, wrap the food for each serving, with a handful of washed seaweed—or spinach if seaweed is not available—and salt and freshly ground pepper, first in cheesecloth, then in foil to make an airtight packet. To cook on the range, place a layer of scrubbed rocks on a wire rack in the bottom of a clam steamer or a four-gallon kettle. Add two cups of water and cook four packets per kettle over medium heat. The packets may also be cooked over a medium hot fire on an outdoor grill. In either case, cook for from fifty minutes to an hour.

However you decide to prepare your clambake, informality should be the keynote. Use large, colorful napkins, even hand towels. If you're using a picnic table, cover it with a washable tablecloth, or even with newspaper and set out earthenware bowls of melted butter. You could use milk crates or nail kegs for seats. And you might fill one of the kegs with draft beer and set it in a tub of ice. Otherwise, serve your guests frosty bottles of cold beer.

You can also serve fresh fish at an outdoor brunch. If you wish to grill a whole fish over hot coals, split it in half, brush it with butter, sprinkle it with salt and pepper to taste, and then lightly flour it. Place it on an oiled grill rack, and broil on each side for about five minutes. Because fish flakes apart easily, turn it only once and baste it often. Top with melted butter and snipped fresh parsley; serve with lemon wedges. For a recipe for grilled whole bass, see page 135.

Kebabs fashioned from cubes of fish are also delicious outdoor fare.

Try the recipe for Sole Kebabs or make kebabs of pieces of halibut. Cut the fish into one-inch cubes, thread them on skewers, and brush them with a marinade made of one part lemon juice to six parts olive oil. Add a pressed garlic clove and salt and pepper to taste. Broil for about five minutes, basting and turning the skewers frequently.

BAKED STRIPED BASS

1	(3- to 4-pound) whole striped bass, dressed and boned	2	cloves garlic
½	teaspoon salt	1	cup thinly sliced fresh mushrooms
⅛	teaspoon pepper	½	cup parsley sprigs
1	shallot, thinly sliced	2	celery stalks, with leaves
¼	cup thinly sliced onion	1	tablespoon butter or margarine
2	bay leaves		
	Pinch dried thyme leaves	3	cups dry white wine

Sauce

Cooking liquid from fish
1 teaspoon plus ½ cup butter or margarine

1 teaspoon all-purpose flour

1. Preheat oven to 400°F. Lightly grease a large, shallow baking pan.
2. Wash bass; pat dry with paper towels.
3. Sprinkle bass, inside and out, with salt and pepper.
4. Place in prepared baking pan. Add remaining ingredients, except Sauce, distributing evenly around bass.
5. Bake, basting frequently with liquid in pan, 40 minutes, or until fish flakes easily with fork.
6. Carefully remove fish to heated serving platter; cover, and keep in warm place.
7. Make Sauce: Strain cooking liquid from fish into small saucepan; discard vegetables. Cook liquid, uncovered and over medium heat, until it measures 1 cup—about 15 to 20 minutes. Remove the liquid from heat.

8. Combine 1 teaspoon butter with flour; blend into hot liquid.

9. Bring to boil, stirring; boil 2 minutes.

10. Reduce heat. Add remaining butter, shaking pan from side to side until butter melts. Then remove the sauce from heat. Pass sauce with fish.

Makes 6 servings.

GRILLED BASS, PROVENÇALE

1 (4-pound) whole striped bass, dressed and split	2 tablespoons chopped fresh tarragon leaves*
4 tablespoons salad or olive oil	1 teaspoon chopped fresh rosemary leaves*
4 tablespoons lemon juice	1 small onion, sliced
1½ teaspoons salt	
¼ teaspoon pepper	
1 small stalk celery with leaves, chopped	Chopped parsley
	Lemon wedges
1½ teaspoons chopped fresh thyme leaves*	

1. Wash fish thoroughly; pat dry inside and out with paper towels.

2. With sharp knife, make 4 diagonal slashes through skin on each side.

3. In small bowl, combine oil and lemon juice. Brush some of mixture over inside of fish; sprinkle with 1 teaspoon salt and the pepper.

4. In small bowl, combine celery, thyme, tarragon, and rosemary. Sprinkle half of mixture over inside of fish; add onion slices in a layer; sprinkle with remaining herb mixture. Close opening with skewers.

5. Add rest of salt to remaining oil mixture. Brush some of mixture over both sides of fish.

---

*Or use ½ teaspoon dried thyme, 2 teaspoons dried tarragon, and ¼ teaspoon dried rosemary.

6. Place fish on a well-oiled grill or in basket, and adjust 5 inches above prepared coals. Cook 15 to 20 minutes, or until fish flakes easily when tested with a fork on underside. Brush with remaining oil mixture. Carefully turn fish with wide spatulas, or turn basket; cook 15 to 20 minutes, or until done.

7. Remove to serving platter. Sprinkle with parsley; garnish with lemon wedges.

Makes 6 servings.

CLAMS OREGANO

2 **dozen clams in shells, well scrubbed**
¾ **cup butter or margarine, melted**
1 **cup packaged dry bread crumbs**
2 **cloves garlic, crushed**
2 **tablespoons chopped parsley**
2 **tablespoons grated Parmesan cheese**

4 **teaspoons lemon juice**
1 **teaspoon dried oregano leaves**
⅛ **teaspoon Tabasco**
Rock salt

Lemon wedges
Parsley sprigs

1. In large kettle, bring ½ inch water to boil. Add clams; simmer, covered, until clams open—6 to 10 minutes.

2. Meanwhile, in medium-size bowl, combine butter with bread crumbs, garlic, chopped parsley, Parmesan, lemon juice, oregano, and Tabasco.

3. Remove the clams from kettle; discard top shells. Remove clams from bottom shells; chop coarsely, and add to crumb mixture. Spoon into bottom shells.

4. Place a layer of rock salt, ½ inch deep, in a large roasting pan or two shallow casseroles; sprinkle with water to dampen.

5. Arrange filled clam shells on salt. Run under broiler just until golden brown—about 5 minutes. Garnish with lemon wedges and parsley sprigs. Serve at once.

Makes 4 servings.

CODFISH CAKES

½ pound salt codfish
1½ cups diced pared potato
1 egg
2 tablespoons cream

⅛ teaspoon pepper
¼ cup butter or margarine

Catsup

1. Soak codfish in cold water 12 hours, or overnight, or as package label directs.
2. Cut into 1-inch-wide strips or small pieces. Place in small saucepan; add water to cover. Bring to boil; reduce heat; simmer, uncovered, 5 minutes. Drain.
3. Meanwhile, in covered medium-size saucepan, cook potato in unsalted water to cover 10 to 15 minutes, or until tender. Drain.
4. Mash potato in saucepan. Beat in egg, cream, and pepper until smooth.
5. With a fork, flake codfish. Add to potato mixture; beat until light and fluffy.
6. Heat butter in large skillet. Spoon cod mixture in 6 mounds into skillet; pat into 1-inch-thick cakes. Cook, over medium heat, 4 or 5 minutes, or until underside is browned. Turn; brown other side 4 or 5 minutes.
7. Serve at once, with catsup.
Makes 3 to 4 servings.

CRABCAKES

1 pound crab meat, or 2 cans (7½-ounce size)
1 medium-size onion
½ cup butter or margarine
1 cup fine dry bread crumbs
3 eggs
1 teaspoon salt

1 teaspoon dry mustard
Few sprigs parsley, chopped
2 tablespoons heavy cream
Flour

Lemon or lime slices

1. Fork crab meat into flakes, if necessary.

2. Chop onion finely, and cook in ¼ cup butter or margarine until limp. Toss in bread crumbs, and mix well.

3. Beat eggs thoroughly; add to crab meat, along with crumb mixture, salt, mustard, chopped parsley, and cream. Shape into 8 flat patties.

4. Coat with flour, and fry in remaining butter until patties are delicately browned on both sides.

5. Serve, with slices of lemon or lime.

Makes 4 servings.

CRAB-MEAT SALAD WITH REMOULADE SAUCE

1½ pounds fresh or frozen
    crab meat
5 stalks celery
1 clove garlic
1½ teaspoons dried tarragon
Few sprigs parsley
2 hard-cooked eggs
2 cups mayonnaise or salad
    dressing

2 tablespoons capers
1 teaspoon anchovy paste
1 teaspoon dry mustard

Watercress
Peeled tomato slices
Cucumber slices

1. Remove all bones and cartilage from crab meat, and divide into sizable flakes.

2. Cut celery in very thin slices. Toss crab meat and celery together. Chill in refrigerator until sauce is made.

3. Crush garlic, or chop very fine, and mix with remaining ingredients, except garnishes.

4. Shortly before serving, mix crab meat with about two thirds of sauce.

5. Transfer to salad platter or bowl, and garnish with watercress, thin slices of peeled tomatoes, and thin slices of cucumber. Serve remaining sauce in a separate bowl.

Makes 6 servings.

CURRIED CRAB-STUFFED AVOCADOS

3 large ripe avocados (about 2¼ pounds)

6 teaspoons lime or lemon juice
Angostura bitters

Curried Crab Meat

1 can (7½ ounces) king-crab meat*
2 tablespoons butter or margarine
½ cup chopped onion
2 to 3 teaspoons curry powder
2 tablespoons flour
½ teaspoon salt

Dash cayenne
¼ cup light cream
½ cup dry white wine or sherry
1 tablespoon lime or lemon juice
½ cup chopped toasted almonds

Paprika

1. Cut avocados in half lengthwise; remove pits. Sprinkle each half with 1 teaspoon lime juice and a few drops bitters; set aside.

2. Preheat oven to 350°F.

3. Make Curried Crab Meat: Drain crab meat; separate, removing any cartilage.

4. In hot butter in medium-size saucepan, sauté onion and curry powder until onion is tender—about 5 minutes.

5. Remove from heat. Add flour, salt, cayenne; stir until smooth. Gradually stir in cream and wine.

6. Over medium heat, bring to boil, stirring constantly. Reduce heat; simmer 1 minute.

7. Remove from heat. Stir in crab meat, 1 tablespoon lime juice, and the almonds, mixing well.

8. Fill each avocado half with about ⅓ cup curried mixture. Sprinkle with paprika.

9. Arrange avocados in a 13- by 9- by 1¾-inch pan. Cover top of pan loosely with foil.

10. Bake avocados 20 minutes. Serve at once.

Makes 6 servings.

---

*Or use 1 package (6 ounces) frozen crab meat, thawed and drained.

SCALLOPED CRAB

1 pound fresh crab meat, or 2 cans (7½-ounce size) crab meat
½ cup dry sherry
¼ cup butter or margarine
2 tablespoons finely chopped onion
¼ cup unsifted all-purpose flour
½ cup milk
1 cup light cream

1 tablespoon Worcestershire sauce
1 teaspoon salt
Dash pepper
2 egg yolks, slightly beaten
2 tablespoons butter or margarine, melted
½ cup packaged dry bread crumbs

1. Preheat oven to 350°F. Lightly grease 6 or 8 scallop shells or a 1-quart casserole.

2. Drain crab meat, removing any cartilage. Sprinkle crab meat with ¼ cup sherry; toss to mix well.

3. In ¼ cup hot butter in medium-size saucepan, sauté onion until tender—5 minutes.

4. Remove from heat. Stir in flour. Gradually stir in milk and cream; bring to boil, stirring; reduce heat, and simmer until quite thick—8 to 10 minutes.

5. Remove from heat; add Worcestershire, salt, pepper, and rest of sherry. Stir a little of sauce into egg yolks; return to rest of sauce in saucepan; mix well. Stir in crab-meat mixture.

6. Turn into shells or casserole.

7. Toss 2 tablespoons butter with crumbs to mix well. (If using casserole, use 1 tablespoon butter and ¼ cup crumbs.) Sprinkle crumbs evenly over crab meat.

8. Place shells on cookie sheet; bake 20 minutes, or until mixture is bubbly and crumbs are lightly browned. (Bake casserole 25 minutes.)

Makes 6 servings.

SHERRIED CRAB BAKE

2 cans (7½-ounce size) crab meat
¼ cup butter or margarine
2 tablespoons all-purpose flour
¼ teaspoon salt
Dash cayenne

Dash paprika
1 cup milk
2 tablespoons finely chopped parsley
¼ cup dry sherry
1 hard-cooked egg, chopped

Topping

1 tablespoon butter or margarine, melted
⅛ teaspoon garlic powder
1 tablespoon finely chopped chives

1½ cups bite-size toasted corn cereal, crushed

1. Preheat oven to 325°F.

2. Lightly grease 6 scalloped baking shells or individual baking dishes.

3. Separate crab-meat pieces into a small bowl, removing membrane; set aside.

4. Melt butter in medium-size saucepan; remove from heat. Add flour, salt, cayenne, and paprika, stirring until smooth. Add milk and parsley; bring to boil, stirring. Reduce heat, and simmer until thickened—about 5 minutes.

5. Remove from heat. Stir in crab meat, sherry, and egg; reheat gently. Spoon into baking shells.

6. Make Topping: Combine all ingredients until well blended. Sprinkle over crab-meat mixture.

7. Place shells on cookie sheet; bake 15 minutes, or until topping is nicely browned.

Makes 6 servings.

BAKED STUFFED WHOLE FISH

Savory Stuffing:
1 egg, beaten
¼ teaspoon dried thyme leaves
½ teaspoon dill seed
2 tablespoons chopped parsley
¼ teaspoon salt
Dash pepper
½ cup butter or margarine, melted
3 tablespoons finely chopped onion
3 cups day-old white-bread crumbs, grated

1 (3- to 5-pound) whole fish, dressed and split (red snapper, bluefish, mackerel, whitefish, cod, haddock, striped bass, or similar fish)
Salt
Pepper
2 tablespoons butter or margarine, melted

4 to 8 lemon wedges

1. Preheat oven to 500°F.
2. Make Savory Stuffing: Combine egg, thyme, dill seed, parsley, salt, and pepper in a large bowl; mix well.
3. In hot butter, sauté the chopped onion until it is golden—about 5 minutes.
4. To the seasonings, add the onion-butter mixture, 2 tablespoons hot water, and bread crumbs, tossing lightly with a fork to mix well.
5. Sprinkle inside of fish with salt and pepper.
6. Place fish in large, shallow baking dish; stuff. Close opening with skewers or toothpicks.
7. Brush top with 2 tablespoons melted butter; then bake, uncovered, for 10 minutes.
8. Reduce heat to 400°F.; bake 10 minutes per pound, or until the fish flakes easily with a fork. Serve with lemon wedges.
Makes 4 to 8 servings.

BAKED HADDOCK, NEW ENGLAND STYLE

1 (3-pound) fresh haddock, cleaned, head and tail removed

1½ teaspoons seasoned salt
Pepper
2 tablespoons lemon juice

Cracker Topping

½ cup crushed unsalted crackers	melted
½ cup chopped, washed fresh mushrooms	2 tablespoons lemon juice
¼ cup thinly sliced green onions	6 slices bacon
2 tablespoons chopped parsley ·	
1½ teaspoons seasoned salt	Parsley (optional)
⅛ teaspoon pepper	Lemon wedges (optional)
¼ cup butter or margarine,	

1. Wash fish in cold water; pat dry with paper towels. With sharp knife, carefully remove bones, keeping fish joined down back. (Or have fish boned at market.)

2. Preheat oven to 400°F. Line a 13- by 9- by 2-inch baking pan with foil; butter foil.

3. Sprinkle inside of boned fish with ¾ teaspoon seasoned salt, dash pepper, and 1 tablespoon lemon juice. Fold fish lengthwise. Place in prepared pan. Sprinkle with ¾ teaspoon seasoned salt, dash pepper, and 1 tablespoon lemon juice.

4. Make Cracker Topping: In medium-size bowl, combine crushed crackers, mushrooms, green onions, parsley, seasoned salt, and pepper; mix. Pour on butter and lemon juice; toss until well combined.

5. Spoon over fish in a 3-inch-wide layer. Arrange bacon slices diagonally over top.

6. Bake, basting every 10 minutes with pan juices, 30 to 35 minutes, or until fish flakes easily when tested with a fork.

7. Carefully lift fish to heated serving platter. Garnish with parsley and lemon wedges, if desired.

Makes 6 servings.

CARIBBEAN LOBSTER SALAD

6 (8-ounce size) frozen rock-lobster tails	⅓ cup mayonnaise
3½ teaspoons salt	½ teaspoon soy sauce
1 bottle (8 ounces) Italian-style salad dressing	Dash pepper
	Dash cayenne

1½ cups fresh pineapple wedges; or 1 can (1 pound, 4½ ounces) pineapple chunks, drained

1½ cups sliced celery

Crisp salad greens
6   lime wedges

1. Bring 3 quarts water to boil. Add unthawed lobster tails and 2 teaspoons salt; return to boiling.

2. Reduce heat; simmer, covered, 10 minutes. Drain; cool.

3. With scissors, cut undershells from lobster tails, reserving shells.

4. Remove lobster meat in one piece; cut into ¾-inch pieces.

5. In medium-size bowl, toss lobster with salad dressing, coating well.

6. Refrigerate, covered, at least 30 minutes, stirring occasionally. Drain; reserve dressing.

7. In large bowl, combine mayonnaise with soy sauce, pepper, cayenne, and remaining salt; blend well.

8. Add lobster, pineapple, and celery, mixing gently. Mound lobster salad in shells. Serve on greens tossed with reserved dressing; garnish with lime wedges.

Makes 6 servings.

COLD LOBSTER WITH HERB HOLLANDAISE SAUCE

1   lemon, sliced
2   medium-size onions, sliced
2   medium-size carrots, cut in 1-inch pieces
2   stalks celery, cut in 1-inch pieces
2   parsley sprigs
2   bay leaves
2   tablespoons salt
8   peppercorns

2   (1½-pound size) live lobsters

Parsley (optional)
Lemon wedges (optional)

Herb Hollandaise Sauce (see p. 145)

1. In deep, 10-quart kettle, combine 4 quarts water, the lemon, onion, carrot, celery, parsley, bay leaves, salt, and peppercorns. Bring to boil; reduce heat; simmer, covered, 20 minutes.

2. Plunge lobsters into kettle, head first. Return water to boiling; reduce heat, and simmer, covered, 10 minutes, or until shells are bright red.

3. Remove kettle from heat. Let lobsters cook 20 minutes longer as liquid cools. Drain; refrigerate, covered.

4. To serve: Place lobster on back; with sharp knife, split body down middle, cutting through thin undershell. Discard dark vein, small sac below head, and spongy tissue. Crack the claws.

5. Arrange lobsters on serving platter; garnish with parsley and lemon wedges, if desired. Serve with Herb Hollandaise Sauce.

Makes 2 servings.

HERB HOLLANDAISE SAUCE

2 egg yolks	1 teaspoon dried tarragon
¼ cup butter or margarine	leaves
1½ tablespoons lemon juice	1 teaspoon chopped parsley
¼ teaspoon salt	

1. In top of double boiler, with wire whisk or electric mixer at low speed, slightly beat egg yolks. Gradually add ¼ cup boiling water, beating constantly. Cook over hot water, beating constantly, just until thickened.

2. Beat in butter, 1 tablespoon at a time, beating well after each addition until butter is melted.

3. Remove double-boiler top from hot water. Beat in lemon juice, salt, tarragon, and parsley.

4. Turn into serving bowl; cover. Refrigerate until chilled. (Sauce may be served at room temperature, if desired.)

Makes ⅔ cup.

DEVILED LOBSTER

1   bay leaf
1   lemon, sliced
1   teaspoon sugar
1   teaspoon salt
3   (8-ounce size) frozen
    rock-lobster tails
1   can (3 ounces) button
    mushrooms

1   tablespoon flour
½   cup milk
½   teaspoon seasoned salt
½   teaspoon soy sauce
1   egg yolk
1   tablespoon dry sherry
1   tablespoon grated Parmesan
    cheese

1. In large saucepan, combine 4 cups water, the bay leaf, lemon slices, sugar, and salt; bring to boil. Add lobster tails; boil gently 10 minutes. Drain.

2. Meanwhile, drain liquid from mushrooms into a 1-cup measure; add water to make ½ cup. Gradually stir into flour in small saucepan. Add milk, seasoned salt, and soy sauce.

3. Bring to boil, stirring constantly. Reduce heat, and simmer 3 minutes.

4. In small bowl, beat egg yolk; gradually stir in hot mixture. Return to saucepan, and cook, stirring, just to boiling point. Remove from heat; stir in wine.

5. Remove lobster meat from shells, being careful to keep shells intact. Cut meat into bite-size pieces. Add, with mushrooms, to sauce; cook over medium heat just until heated through.

6. Spoon into lobster shells. Sprinkle each with 1 teaspoon Parmesan.

7. Broil, 2 inches from heat, just until cheese is golden brown—2 to 3 minutes.

Makes 3 servings.

LOBSTER NEWBURG

¼   cup butter or margarine
2   tablespoons flour
¼   teaspoon salt
¼   teaspoon nutmeg
½   teaspoon paprika
1   cup heavy cream

3   egg yolks, slightly beaten
2   cups coarsely chopped boiled
    lobster
2   tablespoons dry sherry

3   cups hot cooked white rice

1. Melt butter in top of double boiler, over direct heat; remove from heat. Stir in flour to make a smooth mixture. Add salt, nutmeg, and paprika.

2. Gradually stir in cream. Bring to boil, stirring; reduce heat, and simmer, stirring, 3 minutes longer.

3. Stir a little of hot mixture into egg yolks; pour back into top of double boiler. Add lobster; cook, stirring, over hot water, until mixture is thickened and lobster is hot—about 10 minutes. (Do not boil.)

4. Stir in sherry. Serve over rice.

Makes 4 servings.

LOBSTER THERMIDOR

8 (8-ounce size) frozen rock-lobster tails	3 tablespoons sherry
	2 tablespoons brandy

Sauce

½ cup butter or margarine	1½ cups light cream
¼ cup unsifted all-purpose flour	1 egg yolk, slightly beaten
1 teaspoon salt	½ cup grated sharp Cheddar cheese
⅛ teaspoon mace	
Dash paprika	

1. Cook frozen lobster tails as package label directs. Drain; cool quickly in cold water; drain.

2. Remove lobster meat from shells, keeping shells intact. Cut lobster into bite-size pieces.

3. In large bowl, toss lobster with sherry and brandy; cover; set aside.

4. Wash and dry lobster shells; set aside.

5. Preheat oven to 450°F.

6. Make Sauce: Melt butter in large saucepan; remove from heat. Stir in flour, salt, mace, and paprika. Gradually stir in cream.

7. Bring to boil, stirring constantly; reduce heat, and simmer several minutes.

8. Stir some of hot mixture into egg yolk; pour back into saucepan. Add lobster meat.

9. Cook, stirring, over low heat, until sauce is thickened and lobster is heated through.

10. Arrange shells on cookie sheet and fill them with lobster mixture, mounding high. Sprinkle each with 1 tablespoon grated cheese.

11. Bake until cheese is melted and top is golden brown—8 to 10 minutes.

Makes 8 servings.

OYSTER-AND-CHEESE PIE

3 bacon slices
3 eggs, slightly beaten
1 can (10 ounces) frozen condensed oyster stew, thawed
⅓ cup milk

1 cup grated Swiss cheese (¼ pound)
Dash pepper

8-inch baked pie shell, cooled

1. Preheat oven to 350°F.

2. In skillet, sauté bacon until crisp. Drain; crumble.

3. Combine eggs, soup, and milk; mix well. Add the cheese and a dash pepper.

4. Pour half of egg mixture into pie shell; place on rack in oven. Pour rest of egg mixture into shell; sprinkle top with bacon.

5. Bake 35 to 40 minutes, or until firm in center.

Makes 4 to 6 servings.

OYSTERS ROCKEFELLER

1 small onion
1 stalk celery
8 sprigs parsley
½ bunch watercress
1 cup butter or margarine
½ cup dry bread or cracker crumbs
½ teaspoon anise extract*

¼ teaspoon salt
Dash pepper
Dash Tabasco

Rock salt

1½ dozen oysters on the half shell

---

*Or use a pinch of ground anise.

1. Chop onion, celery, parsley, and watercress very fine.
2. Heat ¼ cup butter in skillet.
3. Add chopped vegetables; cook, stirring frequently, until onion is limp. Remove from heat.
4. Stir in remaining ¾ cup butter, crumbs, anise, salt, pepper, and Tabasco. Set aside.
5. Preheat oven to 450°F.
6. Pour a thick layer of rock salt on bottom of shallow baking dish. Dampen salt with sprinkling of water.
7. Pour liquor off oysters. Cover each oyster (still in its half shell) with 1 tablespoon of crumb mixture. Arrange shells on salt, and bake 5 to 8 minutes.

Makes 4 to 6 servings.

OYSTER SAUSAGES

½ pound ground lean lamb
¼ pound suet
¾ cup fresh oysters, or 1 can (7 ounces) frozen

¼ cup light cream
¼ teaspoon pepper
1 teaspoon salt

1. Thoroughly mix ground lamb, finely chopped suet, coarsely chopped oysters, a little oyster liquor, and other ingredients.
2. Shape into rolls about size of link sausage (or into patties).
3. Fry over low heat, keeping skillet covered, about 15 minutes.
4. Remove cover; drain off all fat, and continue frying until nicely browned.

Makes 4 servings.

SALMON MOUSSE

1 envelope unflavored gelatin
2 cans (1-pound size) red salmon
1½ cups diced peeled cucumber
¼ cup lemon juice
½ cup mayonnaise

½ teaspoon salt
6 drops Tabasco
½ cup heavy cream, whipped

Lemon slices (optional)
Parsley (optional)

1. In small saucepan, sprinkle gelatin over ½ cup cold water; heat over low heat, stirring constantly, until gelatin is dissolved. Set aside.

2. Drain salmon; turn into pie plate. Discard any skin and large bones; flake fish.

3. In electric-blender container, combine about one quarter of the salmon and one quarter of cucumber and lemon juice. Blend at high speed until smooth. Pour into large bowl. Repeat until all is used.

4. Stir in mayonnaise, salt, Tabasco, and dissolved gelatin. Fold in whipped cream. Turn into 5-cup fish-shape mold or ring mold.

5. Refrigerate until firm—at least 4 hours.

6. To unmold: Run a small spatula around edge of mold; invert over serving platter; shake gently to release. If necessary, place a hot, damp cloth over mold; shake again to release. Garnish with lemon slices and parsley, if desired.

Makes 6 to 8 servings.

SALMON STEAKS WITH CAPER SAUCE

2 (1¼-pound size) salmon
   steaks
  About 1½ quarts boiling water

¼ teaspoon bouquet garni
3 tablespoons dry white wine

Caper Sauce

1 tablespoon butter or
   margarine
1 tablespoon flour
½ teaspoon salt
6 tablespoons dry white wine
1 tablespoon white-wine
   vinegar

1 egg yolk
2 tablespoons bottled capers,
   drained

Watercress (optional)
Lemon wedges (optional)

1. Wipe salmon with damp paper towels. Place in 2 layers of cheesecloth.

2. In a 3-quart saucepan, combine boiling water, bouquet garni, and 3 tablespoons white wine.

3. Add salmon steaks in cheesecloth; simmer, uncovered, 12 to 15 minutes. (Fish should flake easily with fork.) Drain fish, reserving ½ cup cooking liquid.

4. Make Caper Sauce: Melt butter in small saucepan; remove from heat. Stir in flour and salt; gradually stir in 6 tablespoons white wine, the vinegar, and reserved cooking liquid.

5. Bring to boil, stirring constantly; reduce heat, and simmer several minutes.

6. Stir a little of hot mixture into egg yolk; pour back into saucepan; cook, over low heat, stirring, 2 minutes, or until thickened.

7. Remove from heat. Stir in capers. Place salmon on serving platter. Pour sauce over salmon. Garnish with watercress and lemon wedges, if desired.

Makes 4 servings.

SALMON TIMBALES

1 can (5 ounces) deveined shrimp, drained	1 teaspoon salt
¼ cup butter or margarine	¼ teaspoon pepper
¼ cup unsifted all-purpose flour	2 eggs, slightly beaten
2 cups milk	1 tablespoon sherry
2 cans (7¾-ounce size) salmon, drained	1 tablespoon lemon juice
	½ teaspoon paprika

1. Preheat oven to 350°F.

2. Lightly grease four 6-ounce custard cups. Place 1 shrimp in center of each cup.

3. In medium-size saucepan, melt 2 tablespoons butter. Remove from heat. Add 2 tablespoons flour, stirring until smooth. Gradually stir in ½ cup milk. Bring to boil, stirring constantly. Remove from heat.

4. Flake salmon with fork. Add to milk mixture, with ½ teaspoon salt, pepper, and eggs; mix well. Spoon salmon mixture over shrimp in each cup.

5. Set cups in pan containing 1 inch hot water; bake 35 minutes.

6. Meanwhile, make sauce: Melt rest of butter in medium-size saucepan. Remove from heat.

7. Add rest of flour, stirring until smooth. Gradually stir in rest of milk; bring to boil, stirring constantly. Reduce heat. Add sherry, lemon juice, paprika, and rest of salt.

8. Coarsely chop remaining shrimp. Add to sauce; stir over low heat until hot.

9. Unmold timbales onto warm platter. Top each with some of sauce; pass rest of sauce.

Makes 4 servings.

SCALLOPS WITH LEMON-CHIVE-BUTTER SAUCE

Sauce

3 tablespoons butter or margarine
3 tablespoons lemon juice
⅛ teaspoon seasoned salt
Dash cayenne
1 tablespoon snipped chives

2 tablespoons butter or margarine
1 pound sea scallops, washed and well drained

3 crisp-cooked slices bacon, crumbled

1. Make Sauce: Melt 3 tablespoons butter in small saucepan. Stir in lemon juice, seasoned salt, cayenne, and chives.

2. Heat 2 tablespoons butter in medium-size skillet. Add scallops; sauté, over high heat and stirring, until browned and tender—5 to 8 minutes.

3. Pour sauce over scallops. Turn into serving dish. Sprinkle with bacon.

Makes 3 or 4 servings.

SCALLOPS MORNAY

2 packages (10-ounce size) frozen chopped broccoli

1½ pounds sea scallops, washed and drained

½ cup dry white wine
1 sprig parsley
Milk
2 tablespoons instant minced
   onion
¼ cup butter or margarine
¼ cup unsifted all-purpose flour

½ teaspoon salt
Dash cayenne
1 cup grated natural Swiss
   cheese (4 ounces)
2 tablespoons grated Parmesan
   cheese

1. Preheat oven to 450°F.
2. Cook broccoli, following package-label directions; drain well. Turn into 6 (10-ounce) individual casseroles or soufflé dishes.
3. In medium-size saucepan, combine scallops with wine and parsley; bring to boil. Reduce heat; simmer, uncovered, 5 minutes.
4. Drain scallops, reserving liquid. Cut each scallop in half. Add enough milk to reserved liquid to measure 2½ cups.
5. Sauté onion in hot butter in small saucepan, stirring constantly, until golden brown; remove from heat. Stir in flour, salt, and cayenne. Gradually stir in reserved liquid.
6. Bring to boil, stirring. Add ¾ cup Swiss cheese; cook, stirring constantly, until cheese is melted; remove from heat. Stir in scallops; spoon over broccoli in casseroles.
7. Combine remaining Swiss cheese with the Parmesan; sprinkle over scallop mixture.
8. Bake 10 to 15 minutes, or until golden brown and bubbly.
Makes 6 servings.

SCALLOPS AND MUSHROOMS

2 packages (12-ounce size)
   frozen scallops
½ pound fresh mushrooms

¼ cup dry sherry
4 tablespoons butter or
   margarine

Sauce

2 tablespoons butter or margarine	½ teaspoon bouquet garni
3 tablespoons chopped onion	⅔ cup sauterne
1 clove garlic, crushed	½ cup catsup
2 tablespoons flour	
1 teaspoon salt	4½ cups hot cooked white rice
	1 tablespoon chopped parsley

1. Thaw scallops as package label directs; drain. Cut large scallops in half, cutting against the grain.

2. Wash and drain mushrooms; slice lengthwise. In large bowl, toss mushrooms with scallops and sherry, mixing well. Let stand, covered, 20 minutes.

3. In 4 tablespoons hot butter in large skillet, sauté scallops and mushrooms, over low heat, stirring occasionally during cooking, until scallops are white and firm—12 to 15 minutes.

4. Meanwhile, make Sauce: Melt 2 tablespoons butter in large saucepan. Add onion and garlic; sauté until tender—about 5 minutes.

5. Remove from heat. Stir in flour, salt, and bouquet garni.

6. Drain scallops and mushrooms, reserving cooking liquid. Measure 1⅓ cups, adding water if necessary.

7. Gradually stir cooking liquid, wine, catsup, scallops, and mushrooms into mixture in saucepan. Cook, stirring, over medium heat, until mixture boils and scallops are heated through.

8. To serve: Arrange rice on platter. Spoon sauce over top. Garnish with parsley.

Makes 6 servings.

COQUILLES ST. JACQUES

½ cup dry sherry	¼ cup finely chopped onion
1½ pounds sea scallops, washed and drained	¼ cup unsifted all-purpose flour
	½ cup milk
6 tablespoons butter or margarine	1 cup light cream
	¼ pound mushrooms, sliced

1 tablespoon Worcestershire sauce

Dash pepper

1 cup grated Cheddar cheese (4 ounces)

2 tablespoons butter or margarine, melted

½ cup packaged seasoned cornflake crumbs

1. Preheat oven to 350°F.

2. Pour ¼ cup sherry over scallops; mix well.

3. In 4 tablespoons hot butter in medium-size saucepan, sauté onion until tender—5 minutes. Remove from heat; stir in flour. Gradually stir in milk and cream.

4. Bring to boil, stirring. Reduce heat; simmer, stirring frequently, until quite thick—8 to 10 minutes. Remove from heat.

5. Meanwhile, in 2 tablespoons hot butter in medium-size skillet, sauté mushrooms until golden brown—5 minutes.

6. Add Worcestershire, pepper, cheese, and remaining sherry to sauce; stir until cheese is melted. Stir in scallops in sherry and the mushrooms. Turn into 6 to 8 scallop shells or a 1½-quart casserole.

7. Mix 2 tablespoons melted butter with the cornflake crumbs. (If using casserole, use 1 tablespoon butter and ¼ cup crumbs.) Sprinkle over scallops.

8. Place shells on cookie sheet; bake 20 minutes, or until mixture is bubbly and crumbs are lightly browned. (Bake casserole 25 minutes.)

Makes 6 to 8 appetizer servings.

CURRIED SHRIMP

¼ cup butter or margarine

1 cup chopped onion

2 to 3 teaspoons curry powder

½ teaspoon salt

⅛ teaspoon ginger

⅛ teaspoon chili powder

3 tablespoons flour

1 bottle (8 ounces) clam juice

2 pounds raw shrimp, shelled and deveined

1 tablespoon lemon juice

Hot cooked rice

1. In hot butter in large skillet, sauté onion and curry powder until onion is tender—about 5 minutes. Remove from heat.

2. Add salt, ginger, chili powder, and flour; mix well. Stir in clam juice; bring to boil, stirring. Reduce heat; simmer, covered, 5 minutes.

3. Stir in shrimp and lemon juice; simmer, covered, until the shrimp turn pink and are tender—8 to 10 minutes.

4. Serve with hot cooked rice.

Makes 6 servings.

GRILLED SHRIMP IN THE SHELL

2 **pounds large unshelled fresh shrimp**	4 **cloves garlic, crushed**
½ **cup butter or margarine**	2 **tablespoons coarse salt**
	3 **tablespoons chopped parsley**

1. Wash shrimp under cold water; break off feelers, leaving shrimp in shell. Place in large bowl.

2. Melt butter in small saucepan or skillet. Stir in garlic. Pour over shrimp. Sprinkle with salt and 1 tablespoon parsley; toss until shrimp are well coated.

3. To cook on outdoor grill: Place on grill 4 inches above hot coals. Grill 7 minutes; turn; grill 7 minutes longer, or until shrimp are pink and shells are browned. To cook indoors: Place on rack of broiler pan; broil, 4 inches from heat, 6 minutes on each side, or until golden brown.

4. Serve at once, sprinkled with remaining parsley.

Makes 6 servings.

MOLDED SHRIMP SALAD

2 **envelopes unflavored gelatin**	1 **cup mayonnaise**
Ice cubes	½ **cup chili sauce**
1½ **cups yogurt**	2 **tablespoons lemon juice**

2 tablespoons finely chopped green onion
1 teaspoon salt
¼ teaspoon dried tarragon leaves

2 pounds shelled, deveined shrimp, cooked
½ cup chopped celery

Lettuce

1. Sprinkle gelatin over 1½ cups cold water in medium-size saucepan; let soften—about 5 minutes. Bring to boil, stirring until gelatin is dissolved.

2. Set pan in a bowl of ice cubes until gelatin is cold; stir once or twice.

3. Add yogurt, mayonnaise, chili sauce, lemon juice, onion, salt, and tarragon to gelatin; mix until well blended. Refrigerate, or place over ice, stirring occasionally, until mixture is consistency of unbeaten egg white.

4. Set aside and refrigerate 8 shrimp, for garnish. Cut remaining shrimp in ¼-inch pieces. Add chopped shrimp and celery to yogurt mixture; mix well. Turn into a chilled 2-quart mold or 8 individual molds.

5. Refrigerate until set—about 6 hours or overnight.

6. To serve: Unmold onto crisp lettuce. Garnish edge with whole shrimp.

Makes 8 servings.

SOLE KEBABS

4 sole or halibut fillets (about 1 pound)
¼ teaspoon salt
¼ teaspoon paprika
8 cherry tomatoes
8 small fresh mushrooms
8 pitted ripe olives

2 tablespoons butter or margarine, melted
2 teaspoons lemon juice

Parsley (optional)
Lemon wedges (optional)

1. Rinse fish under cold running water; dry on paper towels. Sprinkle with salt and paprika.

2. Fold fillets in half lengthwise. Arrange each on skewer with 2 tomatoes, 2 mushrooms, and 2 olives.

3. Combine butter and lemon juice.

4. Place skewers on greased broiler rack; brush with some of lemon butter. Broil, 3 inches from heat, 5 minutes. Turn, and brush with remaining lemon butter. Broil 5 minutes longer, or until fish flakes easily when tested with a fork.

5. Carefully remove kebabs from broiler rack, and place on serving plate. If desired, garnish with parsley and lemon wedges.

Makes 4 servings.

MOUSSE OF SOLE WITH LOBSTER NEWBURG

1½ pounds sole fillets

Lobster Filling

3 tablespoons butter or margarine	2 cups cubed cooked lobster
¼ cup flour	¼ cup flour
¾ teaspoon salt	1½ teaspoons salt
1¼ cups light cream	⅛ teaspoon white pepper
⅓ cup dry sherry	2 egg whites
1 can (3 ounces) whole mushrooms, drained	1¾ cups light cream
1 tablespoon catsup	Watercress (optional)
2 egg yolks	Lemon (optional)

1. Rinse sole; pat dry with paper towels. Cut each fillet into 4 to 6 strips. Put through meat grinder, using finest blade, 4 times. Place in large bowl of electric mixer; refrigerate, covered, 30 minutes. Generously grease a 2-quart metal charlotte mold, 7 inches in diameter; refrigerate.

2. Meanwhile, make Lobster Filling: Melt the butter in a medium-size saucepan. Remove from heat.

3. Stir in ¼ cup flour and ¾ teaspoon salt until well blended. Gradually stir in 1 cup cream. Bring to boil, stirring constantly; reduce heat, and simmer 1 minute. Stir in sherry, mushrooms, and catsup; cook, over medium heat, until hot.

4. Beat egg yolks with ¼ cup cream. Stir into sauce mixture, along with lobster; cook, stirring, 1 minute. Remove from heat.

5. Add flour, salt, and pepper to ground sole; stir until well blended. With electric beater at medium speed, beat in egg whites. Gradually beat in 1¾ cups cream, 2 tablespoons at a time—takes about 10 minutes. Mixture should be smooth and stiff.

6. Preheat oven to 325°F.

7. Set aside 1 cup sole mixture. Use remaining mixture to line bottom and side of prepared mold to within 1 inch of top. Reserve 1 cup lobster filling; refrigerate. Use remaining filling to fill lined mold. Cover with reserved sole mixture, spreading to edge of mold.

8. Cover mold loosely with greased waxed paper. Place in roasting pan; pour boiling water to 2-inch level around mold.

9. Bake 45 to 50 minutes, or until firm at edge when gently pressed with fingertip.

10. About 10 minutes before mousse is done, heat reserved Lobster Filling over hot water.

11. To serve: Loosen mousse around side with small spatula. Invert onto heated serving platter; lift off mold. Spoon heated filling over top. Garnish with watercress and lemon, if desired. To serve, cut into wedges, and serve with sauce.

Makes 8 servings.

TROUT AMANDINE

3 pounds trout fillets	2 tablespoons lemon juice
½ cup butter or margarine	
¼ cup sliced blanched almonds	Chopped parsley

1. Rinse trout; pat dry with paper towels.

2. Heat ¼ cup butter in large skillet until very hot. Add fillets, and brown on each side—about 3 minutes per side. Remove to warm platter; keep warm.

3. Add remaining butter to skillet; heat. Add almonds; sauté until well browned. Stir in lemon juice. Pour over trout. Sprinkle with parsley.

Makes 4 servings.

BAKED TROUT AND BACON

3 (¾-pound size) fresh rainbow trout, cleaned and split; or 3 frozen trout, thawed
8 slices bacon
1 teaspoon salt
¼ teaspoon pepper
2 tablespoons chopped parsley

1. Preheat oven to 375°F.
2. Wash trout well under running cold water. Drain; pat dry with paper towels.
3. Line a 13- by 9- by 2-inch baking pan with bacon slices; lay trout on bacon. Sprinkle with salt, pepper, and 1 tablespoon parsley.
4. Cover dish with foil, sealing tightly around edge.
5. Bake 20 to 25 minutes, or just until fish flakes easily when tested with a fork.
6. Gently lift trout and bacon to heated serving platter. Sprinkle with remaining parsley.

Makes 6 servings.

7

VEGETABLES

Vegetables make particularly good accompaniments—or even main dishes—for a light brunch. Mushrooms, tomatoes, eggplant, corn, asparagus, and potatoes can be used in many creative ways, as you will see in the selection of recipes that follow.

Corn dishes—hominy, johnnycake, spoonbread, and Mark Twain's favorite, hoecake—became breakfast staples when the Pilgrims settled in America. If you are planning an outdoor brunch, you can save time by roasting the corn at the same time you cook the meat. To prepare corn for roasting, pull the husks down far enough to remove the silk; then replace the husks and fill them with water. Drain by twisting the tops of the husks, and then bake them over hot coals for from twenty to twenty-five minutes. (Always refrigerate corn, with husks on, until ready to use.) For an indoor brunch, prepare an elegant corn soufflé (see page 164), topped with cinnamon and sugar. Serve with a meat platter, warm rolls, and homemade jam.

The exotic *mushroom* makes a fine accompaniment to any brunch. Over thirty-eight thousand varieties of mushrooms have been identified, yet only fifty of them are edible. Of these, only the field mushroom is readily available in most markets throughout the United States.

Fresh mushrooms are always preferable to canned. When you have brought them home from the market, place them loosely into an uncovered container—unwashed—and refrigerate. When you are ready to use them, merely wipe them with a damp cloth to remove the dirt. Do not peel them as most of their flavor is contained within the skin. If you are using them as a garnish, sprinkle them with lemon juice to keep them from darkening.

Carefully selected *tomatoes*—plump, firm, unblemished, and vine-ripened for flavor—either baked or grilled make pretty and tasty companions to almost any brunch dish. They also make colorful garnishes and casements for salads, such as a shrimp or lobster salad. Tomatoes are best kept at room temperature in order to preserve their flavor and high vitamin C content. The skin of a tomato contains many highly valued vitamins, but if you decide that you prefer the delicacy of a skinned tomato, you may easily remove the skin by scraping the tomato with the dull side of a knife until the skin puckers and can be lifted off. Plunging the tomatoes into boiling water for several seconds first softens the skin and makes it even easier to remove. Very often, skinned tomatoes are preferable for use as a salad case. Cut off the tops of the tomatoes, hollow the insides, and allow them to drain for twenty minutes upside down on a rack. They may be stuffed with any seafood salad, deviled eggs, avocado chunks, or curried shrimp—and garnished with mint leaves, black olives, or pimiento shapes.

Eggplant is a versatile vegetable that can be prepared in many interesting ways. Try it French-fried or curried (see recipes on page 165) as a side dish or in a hearty Italian casserole as a main course. Since eggplants contain a great deal of water, the excess must be removed, either by salting and then draining the slices or by stacking them, covering them with a plate, and then pressing them with a heavy weight. The graceful lines of the eggplant and its deep glossy purple skin topped with green leaves make it equally serviceable as a center-piece or as a casing for other food.

The *potato,* or "earth apple," was a staple of the Inca civilization when it was discovered by the Spanish conquistadors in the sixteenth century. The Spanish preferred the variety known as the sweet potato, which they called *batata.* Hence the English word *potato.* The Spaniards introduced the vegetable to Germany, but it took nearly two hundred years for the white potato to become popular in Europe, and it wasn't until the Irish migration in the nineteenth century that it appeared in North America. Today the potato is in close competition with rice and wheat as the world's largest crop.

Potato dishes can make very pleasing accompaniments to any brunch entrée—from eggs to boiled lobster. Choose potatoes with care, avoiding those with uneven shapes, spongy or leathery textures, and greenish skins. Only the finest vegetables should be used to prepare dishes such as French fries and Casserole au Gratin (see page 171).

Asparagus is rather expensive in comparison to other vegetables but its taste and the versatility of preparation make it well worth the extra cost. Special care should be taken when selecting and preparing it. If you are shopping for fresh asparagus, look for smooth stalks of an even color extending almost to the bottom. Avoid asparagus with tips that are open, a sign of aging. Do not be concerned with the size of the stalk—size never affects the quality of the vegetable.

Because asparagus is grown in sandy soil, it is important to remove carefully the scales from the stalks. Then, holding the stalk with both hands, bend it until it snaps. Discard the stem ends. Wash the spears under cold water quickly but thoroughly. The asparagus is now ready for cooking or marinating. If you wish to cook the spears, tie them into a bundle and stand them in a pot of boiling water covering just the lower third of the stalks. Cover the pot and let cook about eight minutes. Serve with lemon and butter or Hollandaise Sauce. If you wish to marinate asparagus, see page 164 for a recipe. If you are using frozen asparagus, prepare it according to the directions on the package.

There are many other vegetables suitable for brunch. *Artichokes,* for example, are decorative as well as tasty and fun to eat. Choose well-formed, firm artichokes of a green, not a brownish, color. Wash them well; with a sharp knife, remove base; using scissors, cut off the top inch or so of the entire artichoke. Stand the artichoke in a deep saucepan filled with several inches of boiling water. Add salt, cover, and boil for about forty-five minutes, or until a leaf can be easily removed. At this point, remove the artichoke from the water and turn it upside down to drain. Serve with small bowls of melted butter or lemon butter. To eat, remove a leaf at a time with your fingers, dip it into the butter, and suck the fleshy part from the leaf. Eat the heart of the artichoke with a knife and fork.

Fresh *broccoli* spears are also appropriate for brunch. Lay them flat in a large skillet, add an inch of water, cover, and allow them to boil for fifteen minutes. *Brussels sprouts* are an equally good brunch dish. They should be boiled in an inch of salted water for about ten minutes.

For variety in your menu planning, several recipes for vegetable salad platters and for vegetable-based soups have been included.

MARINATED ASPARAGUS

6 tablespoons olive oil	⅛ teaspoon Tabasco
3 tablespoons vinegar	1 small onion, thinly sliced
¼ teaspoon pepper	1 clove garlic
¼ teaspoon salt	2 dozen asparagus spears,
½ teaspoon sugar	cooked (see page 163)

1. Combine olive oil, vinegar, pepper, salt, sugar, and Tabasco. Blend well.
2. Add sliced onion and garlic clove.
3. Pour over asparagus and place in refrigerator, covered, for several hours.
Makes 6 servings.

SOUFFLÉED CORN

6 ears fresh corn*	1½ teaspoons baking powder
½ cup butter or margarine	
½ cup sugar	1 tablespoon butter or
1 tablespoon flour	margarine, melted
½ cup evaporated milk, undiluted	¼ cup sugar
	½ teaspoon cinnamon
2 eggs, well beaten	

1. Preheat oven to 350°F. With a sharp knife, cut corn from ears (4 cups), and set aside.
2. In medium-size saucepan, heat ½ cup butter with ½ cup sugar until butter is melted. Stir in flour until well blended. Remove from heat.

---

*Or use 2 cans (12-ounce size) whole-kernel corn.

3. Gradually stir in milk. Add eggs and baking powder; mix well. Fold in corn. Turn into buttered 1-quart casserole.

4. Bake 40 minutes, or until knife inserted in center comes out clean. Brush with melted butter. Sprinkle with sugar and cinnamon.

Makes 6 to 8 servings.

CURRIED EGGPLANT

1 medium-size eggplant (1¼ pounds)	1 teaspoon salt
¼ cup salad oil	¼ teaspoon dry mustard
1 cup chopped onion	Dash cayenne
¼ clove garlic, crushed	½ cup flaked coconut
2 to 3 teaspoons curry powder	1 large green pepper, chopped

1. Wash eggplant. Do not peel. Cut into 1-inch cubes.

2. In hot oil in medium-size skillet, sauté onion, garlic, and curry powder, stirring, until golden—about 5 minutes.

3. Add eggplant, salt, mustard, and cayenne; mix well. Simmer, covered, 10 minutes.

4. Add coconut, green pepper, and 1 cup water; bring to boil. Reduce heat; simmer, covered, 15 minutes, or just until green pepper is tender.

Makes 6 to 8 servings.

FRENCH-FRIED EGGPLANT

2 medium-size eggplant (3½ inches in diameter)	Salad oil or shortening for deep-frying

Batter

1 cup unsifted all-purpose flour	1 tablespoon salad oil
1 teaspoon baking powder	
½ teaspoon salt	Salt (optional)
Dash pepper	
2 eggs, well beaten	Pimiento strips
⅔ cup cold milk	Watercress sprigs

1. Wash eggplant; do not peel. Cut crosswise into slices ½ inch thick. With round or scalloped 3-inch cookie cutter, cut out shapes from eggplant slices.

2. Meanwhile, in electric skillet or deep-fat fryer, slowly heat oil (at least 1½ inches) to 375°F. on deep-frying thermometer.

3. Make Batter: Sift flour, baking powder, salt, and pepper together into medium-size bowl.

4. In a 2-cup measure, combine eggs, milk, and 1 tablespoon salad oil.

5. Gradually add milk mixture to flour mixture, beating with electric mixer until smooth and well combined.

6. Dip eggplant slices into batter, coating completely.

7. Shake off excess batter. Deep-fry 2 minutes on each side, or just until golden brown. (Fry only enough at one time to fit easily into skillet.)

8. Remove with slotted spoon; drain on paper towels. Keep warm in very low oven while frying rest. Sprinkle with salt, if desired.

9. To serve, garnish platter with pimiento strips and watercress sprigs. Makes 6 servings.

FRENCH ONION SOUP

½ cup butter or margarine
8 cups thinly sliced onion
8 cans (10½-ounce size) beef
   bouillon, undiluted
2 teaspoons salt
8 to 10 French-bread slices, cut
   1 inch thick
¼ cup grated Parmesan cheese

1. Heat butter in large skillet.

2. Add onion, and sauté, stirring, until golden—about 8 minutes.

3. Combine sautéed onion, bouillon, and salt in medium-size saucepan; bring to boil.

4. Reduce heat, and simmer, covered, 30 minutes.

5. Meanwhile, toast French-bread slices in broiler until browned on both sides.

6. Sprinkle a side of each with some of grated cheese; run under broiler about 1 minute, or until cheese is bubbly.

7. To serve: Pour the soup into a tureen or into individual soup bowls.

8. Float the toast, cheese side up, on top of the soup.

Makes 8 to 10 servings.

GAZPACHO ANDALUZ

2 to 3 large tomatoes, peeled (1¾ pounds)
1 large cucumber, pared and halved
1 medium-size onion, halved
1 medium-size green pepper, quartered and seeded
1 pimiento, drained
2 cans (12-ounce size) tomato juice

⅓ cup olive or salad oil
⅓ cup red-wine vinegar
¼ teaspoon Tabasco
1½ teaspoons salt
⅛ teaspoon coarsely ground black pepper
2 cloves garlic, split
½ cup packaged croutons

¼ cup chopped chives

1. In electric blender, combine one tomato, half the cucumber, half the onion, a green-pepper quarter, the pimiento, and ½ cup tomato juice. Blend, covered and at high speed, 30 seconds, to purée the vegetables.

2. In a large bowl, mix the puréed vegetables with remaining tomato juice, ¼ cup olive oil, the vinegar, Tabasco, salt, and black pepper.

3. Refrigerate mixture, covered, until it is well chilled—about 2 hours. At the same time, refrigerate 6 serving bowls.

4. Meanwhile, rub inside of small skillet with garlic; reserve garlic. Add rest of oil; heat. Sauté the croutons in oil until they are browned. Set aside until serving time.

5. Chop separately remaining tomato, cucumber, onion, and green pepper. Place each of these, and the croutons, in separate bowls. Serve as accompaniments.

6. Just before serving time, crush reserved garlic. Add to chilled soup, mixing well. Sprinkle with chopped chives. Serve the gazpacho in chilled bowls. Pass the accompaniments.

Makes 6 servings.

MUSHROOMS AND BACON

1½ pounds fresh mushrooms
4 sprigs parsley, chopped
½ teaspoon grated onion
1 teaspoon finely chopped
   green pepper
½ teaspoon salt
Dash pepper
Dash nutmeg
Dash thyme

1 teaspoon Tabasco
1 cup boiling water
1 tablespoon lemon juice, fresh,
   frozen, or canned
3 tablespoons dry sherry

12 slices bacon
Hot buttered toast

1. Preheat oven to 350°F.

2. Wipe mushrooms with damp cloth, or wash quickly in cold water. Pull out stems, and arrange caps in well-buttered baking dish.

3. Coarsely chop stems (snip off tips), and mix with chopped parsley, onion, green pepper, salt, pepper, nutmeg, and thyme. Scatter over caps.

4. Mix Tabasco with 1 cup boiling water, lemon juice, and sherry; pour over mushroom mixture. Cover, and bake 25 to 30 minutes.

5. To serve: Fry or broil bacon until crisp; drain on paper towels. Spoon mushroom mixture over hot buttered toast. Serve crisp bacon on the side.

Makes 6 servings.

MARINATED MUSHROOMS

Salt
1 pound fresh button
   mushrooms
¼ cup chopped onion
1 small clove garlic, finely
   chopped
2 tablespoons chopped parsley
1 bay leaf

Dash pepper
⅛ teaspoon dried tarragon
   leaves
½ cup dry white wine
¼ cup white vinegar
2 tablespoons olive oil
1 teaspoon lemon juice

1. Add 1 teaspoon salt to 3 cups cold water. Wash mushrooms in this; drain.

2. Combine remaining ingredients and ¼ teaspoon salt in large saucepan. Add mushrooms; bring to boiling point.

3. Then reduce heat, and simmer, covered, 8 to 10 minutes, or until mushrooms are tender. Cool.

4. Refrigerate, covered, in marinade at least 2 hours, or until ready to use. Drain just before serving.

Makes 4 servings.

SAVORY STUFFED MUSHROOMS

12 to 16 fresh medium-size mushrooms

½ cup butter or margarine

3 tablespoons finely chopped green pepper

3 tablespoons finely chopped onion

1½ cups fresh bread cubes (¼ inch)

½ teaspoon salt

⅛ teaspoon pepper

Dash cayenne

1. Preheat oven to 350°F.

2. Wipe mushrooms with damp cloth. Remove stems, and chop stems fine; set aside.

3. Heat 3 tablespoons butter in large skillet. Sauté mushroom caps only on bottom side 2 to 3 minutes; remove. Arrange, rounded side down, in shallow baking pan.

4. Heat rest of butter in same skillet. Sauté chopped mushroom stems, green pepper, and onion until tender—about 5 minutes.

5. Remove from heat. Stir in bread cubes and seasonings. Use to fill mushroom caps, mounding mixture high in center.

6. Bake 15 minutes.

Makes 6 to 8 servings.

MUSHROOMS TAMARA

1½ pounds fresh mushrooms
2 large onions
½ cup salad oil
2 tablespoons butter or margarine

1 cup dairy sour cream
2 teaspoons salt
Dash pepper

1. Wipe mushrooms with damp cloth, or wash quickly in cold water. Snip off tips of stems; slice mushrooms, and set aside.
2. Chop onions very fine, and cook in heated oil until limp and golden.
3. Stir in mushrooms, along with butter; cook over moderate heat until tender—about 5 minutes.
4. Reduce heat; stir in sour cream; season with salt and pepper.
Makes 6 servings.

MUSHROOMS WITH TARRAGON

1½ pounds fresh mushrooms
¼ cup butter or margarine
¼ cup olive or salad oil
2 teaspoons salt
¼ teaspoon pepper
¼ teaspoon dried tarragon

1½ cups heavy cream
1 teaspoon lemon juice, fresh, frozen, or canned

Hot toast

1. Wipe mushrooms with damp cloth, or wash quickly in cold water. Snip off tips of stems; cut mushrooms in half lengthwise.
2. Cook in mixture of melted butter and oil 5 minutes. Season with salt, pepper, and tarragon.
3. Stir in heavy cream and lemon juice; cover, and cook very gently 5 minutes more.
4. Serve over hot toast.
Makes 6 servings.

CASSEROLE OF POTATOES AU GRATIN

1½ cups light cream
 2 pounds new potatoes, pared
    and thinly sliced
 1 teaspoon salt

Pepper
 1 cup grated Gruyère cheese (6
    ounces)

1. Preheat oven to 350°F. In small saucepan, heat cream just until bubbles form around edge of pan.

2. Pour ¼ cup cream into a 1-quart shallow baking dish. Arrange one third potatoes in dish; sprinkle with one third salt, dash pepper, and one third cheese; add one third of remaining cream. Repeat twice, using rest of ingredients.

3. Set baking dish in shallow pan. Pour hot water to 1-inch level around dish.

4. Bake 30 minutes, covered. Then bake, uncovered, 1 hour longer, or until potatoes are tender.

Makes 8 servings.

FRENCH-FRIED POTATOES
(Two-step method)

Idaho potatoes
Salad oil or shortening for
   deep-frying

Salt

1. Pare as many Idaho potatoes as desired. Cut lengthwise into ⅜-inch-thick slices. Then cut slices into strips, ⅜ inch wide. Rinse in cold water; drain well on paper towels.

2. Meanwhile, in electric skillet or deep-fat fryer, slowly heat salad oil (1½ to 2 inches) to 360°F. on deep-frying thermometer.

3. In bottom of fryer basket, make a single layer of potatoes. Lower basket slowly into fat; fry potatoes 4 minutes, or until tender but not browned.

4. Remove potatoes; drain well on paper towels. Keep potatoes at room temperature until ready to complete cooking; reserve oil.

5. A few minutes before serving, reheat oil to 375°F. on deep-frying thermometer.

6. Cover bottom of fryer basket with 2 layers of potatoes. Fry 1 minute, or until potatoes are golden.

7. Remove potatoes; drain well on paper towels. Sprinkle with salt. Keep warm in oven while frying rest of potatoes. Serve hot.

FRENCH-FRIED POTATOES
(One-step method)

1. Fill large skillet or deep-fat fryer one third full with salad oil; slowly heat to 375°F. on deep-frying thermometer.

2. Meanwhile, pare 3 large baking potatoes (about 2 pounds); cut lengthwise into quarters.

3. Fry potatoes, a single layer at a time, in hot oil about 10 minutes, or until golden brown and tender.

4. Drain on paper towels. Keep warm.

CRISPY POTATO PUFFS

1 package (8 ounces) frozen French-fried potato puffs
3 tablespoons butter or margarine, melted

4 tablespoons grated Parmesan cheese, or 3 tablespoons packaged seasoned cornflake crumbs

1. Preheat oven to 425°F.

2. Roll the frozen puffs in melted butter, then in cheese, coating evenly.

3. Place the puffs on an ungreased cookie sheet. Bake 12 minutes, or until golden.

4. Serve puffs hot, as an hors d'oeuvre or a vegetable.

Makes 3 servings.

BAKED CHEESE-STUFFED TOMATOES

4 large tomatoes (2½ pounds)
2 cups grated Swiss cheese
½ cup light cream
2 egg yolks, slightly beaten
2 tablespoons snipped chives
3 tablespoons grated onion
½ teaspoon dried marjoram
  leaves

1 teaspoon dry mustard
1½ teaspoons salt

⅓ cup packaged dry bread
  crumbs
2 tablespoons butter or
  margarine, melted

1. Preheat oven to 350°F. Lightly grease a 12- by 8- by 2-inch baking dish.
2. Halve tomatoes crosswise. Scoop out pulp, leaving shells intact. Chop pulp coarsely.
3. Combine tomato pulp with cheese, cream, egg yolks, chives, onion, marjoram, mustard, and salt; mix well.
4. Spoon cheese mixture into tomato shells. Toss bread crumbs with the melted butter; sprinkle over cheese mixture.
5. Arrange tomato halves in prepared dish. Bake 25 minutes, or until tomatoes are tender.
  Makes 8 servings.

BAKED TOMATO HALVES

1 large tomato (about ½
  pound)
2 tablespoons butter or
  margarine
2 tablespoons finely chopped
  onion

½ teaspoon prepared mustard
¼ teaspoon Worcestershire
  sauce
1 slice white bread, torn into
  coarse crumbs
1 teaspoon chopped parsley

1. Preheat oven to 350°F. Wash tomato, and remove stem. Cut in half crosswise. Place, cut side up, in small, shallow baking pan.

2. In 1 tablespoon hot butter in small skillet, sauté onion until tender. Stir in mustard and Worcestershire. Spread on tomato halves.

3. Melt remaining butter in same skillet. Stir in bread crumbs and parsley. Sprinkle over tomatoes.

4. Bake, uncovered, 20 minutes, or until tomato is heated through and crumbs are golden brown.

Makes 2 servings.

TOMATOES PROVENÇALE

5 medium-size tomatoes	2 tablespoons finely chopped
Prepared mustard	parsley
Seasoned salt	Olive or salad oil
1 cup soft bread crumbs	

1. Preheat oven to 450°F. Lightly grease a shallow baking pan.

2. Wash tomatoes; cut in half.

3. Arrange tomato halves, cut side up, in prepared pan. Spread lightly with mustard. Sprinkle with seasoned salt.

4. Combine bread crumbs and parsley; sprinkle over tomatoes. Drizzle a little oil over each.

5. Bake 10 to 15 minutes, or until bread-crumb mixture is golden.

Makes 10 servings.

SAUTÉED TOMATOES

2 tomatoes	¼ teaspoon salt
2 tablespoons butter or	Dash pepper
margarine	1 teaspoon sugar
½ teaspoon dried basil leaves	

1. Wash tomatoes; cut out core, and cut in quarters.

2. In medium-size skillet, melt butter over low heat. Add tomatoes; sprinkle with basil, salt, and pepper; sauté 5 minutes.

3. With slotted spatula, turn tomatoes. Sprinkle with sugar; sauté 3 minutes longer, or until cooked through.

Makes 4 servings.

TOSSED GREEN SALAD BOWL

1 medium-size head Boston lettuce
½ pound young spinach
½ small head chicory

1 small cucumber
4 radishes

French dressing (see below)

1. Wash greens thoroughly; drain well. Core lettuce; break leaves in bite-size pieces into large salad bowl. Remove stems from spinach, and discard; break leaves into salad bowl. Break chicory to measure 2 cups, and add.

2. Thinly slice cucumber and radishes; add to greens. Cover bowl; refrigerate until serving time.

3. Prepare French dressing.

4. Just before serving, shake dressing well; pour over salad. Toss until greens are well coated.

Makes 8 servings.

FRENCH DRESSING

1 cup salad oil
½ cup olive oil
¼ cup dry white wine
½ cup red-wine vinegar
2 teaspoons salt

½ teaspoon pepper
½ teaspoon dry mustard
½ teaspoon dried basil leaves
½ cup chopped parsley
1 clove garlic, finely chopped

1. Combine all ingredients in medium-size bowl; beat, with rotary beater, until well blended.

2. Pour into jar with tight-fitting lid. Refrigerate at least 2 hours. Shake well just before serving.

Makes 2½ cups.

MARINATED VEGETABLE SALAD PLATTER

1 package (9 ounces) frozen artichoke hearts

1 bottle (8 ounces) Italian-style dressing

1 can (1 pound) whole green beans, drained

1 can (1 pound) small whole beets, drained

1 can (15 ounces) green asparagus, drained

1 can (15 ounces) white asparagus, drained

1 can (12 ounces) julienne carrots, drained

1 tablespoon finely chopped onion

½ teaspoon dried basil leaves

1 large tomato

1 tablespoon chopped parsley

1. Cook artichoke hearts as package label directs; drain. Turn into a bowl; toss with 3 tablespoons dressing. Cover; refrigerate 4 hours.

2. Meanwhile, in large, shallow baking dish, arrange drained green beans, beets, asparagus, and carrots in separate mounds.

3. Sprinkle vegetables with onion and basil. Spoon remaining dressing over vegetables, to coat well. Cover; refrigerate 4 hours.

4. To serve: Slice the tomato. Then arrange slices attractively, with other vegetables, on a large platter. Spoon over them any dressing left in baking dish. Sprinkle white asparagus with chopped parsley.

Makes 8 servings.

8

BREADS AND BUTTERS

BREAD

The art of bread-making is enjoying a revival in America today. Housewives have recently become aware of the low vitamin and mineral content of commercially processed breads, and many women have decided to bake their own, using unmilled whole grains, honey as a natural sweetener, and wholesome additions such as raisins and nuts.

Bread has been considered the staff of life in every civilization since the dawn of man. Each civilization has developed its particular variety of the delicious staple. Since America is the great melting pot, a vast number of different types of bread are commercially available here, particularly in the ethnic sections of large cities. There is sour dough, once popular in the Northwest lumber camps, Irish soda bread, steaming New England brown bread, pumpernickel, Arabian pita bread, Slavic potato bread, long loaves of French and Italian bread, Jewish bagels, Swedish limpa, Russian black bread, and the many varieties of our own cornbread. You can serve any of these superb breads with your brunch, with a choice of cheeses—the soft varieties combine especially well with bread as do cold meats or unsalted butter and homemade jams.

Cheese Bread (see page 183) is a delightful choice for brunch because it is light, flavorful, and offers a taste change to many of the popular sweeter brunch dishes. Popovers (see page 189). Poppy-Seed Crescents and Sesame-Seed Rolls (see page 190), Onion Rolls (see page 192), and Salt Crescents (see page 190) are also good accompaniments to a meal. If you are planning a brunch with a menu suitable for breakfast, choose one of the many recipes given for sweet rolls, sweet breads, and coffeecakes. Bread-baking requires no special equipment, though a thermometer to test the temperature of the water and a wire rack for cooling are helpful.

Your own homemade breads will not look like those bought from the bakery, though they will undoubtedly taste far better. A bit of yellow food coloring will enhance the appearance, and a sprinkling of nuts, coconut, citron, almond paste, and grated citrus fruit peels will add to the taste. Or you might like to substitute a layer of jam or thinly sliced, sweetened apples for the fillings suggested here. For a variation from the traditional loaf-pan shape, bake your breads in large coffee cans or small juice cans.

BUTTER

To give your brunch breads, rolls, coffeecakes, pancakes, and waffles a professional touch, serve them with butter curls or molds. The effect will be well worth the effort.

Butter Curls

These delicate snail-like shapes topping a waffle or placed alongside sweet rolls are as practical as they are pretty. The butter can be spread quite easily when shaped into a thin, circular shell. An inexpensive butter curler is the only utensil necessary.

Let the butter curler stand in hot water at least ten minutes before using it. Keep the butter refrigerated; if you are using margarine, it should be frozen. Hold the curler at a forty-five-degree angle. Beginning at the far side of a four-ounce bar of butter, draw the curler lightly and quickly toward you, to make curls. (Dip the curler into hot water each time.) Drop the curls into ice water; refrigerate them, covered, until ready to use.

Note: For larger curls, use a pound block of butter or margarine.

Butter Molds

The butter or margarine should be soft enough to be pliable but not too soft. Scald the wooden or metal molds in boiling water to cover; then chill them in ice water fifteen minutes. Drain the molds, leaving a slight film of water inside each. To fill a wooden mold: With the back of a metal spoon, press the butter firmly into the mold to make a one-quarter-inch thick layer, pushing down hard to force out any air bubbles and to make indentations. Continue to add butter, pressing and smoothing with the back of the spoon, until the block is filled almost to the top. Immerse the mold in ice water five minutes. Remove, shaking off excess water.

To unmold: Run a small metal spatula between the butter and the wooden block. Push the mold out of the block. Gently remove wooden design. If necessary, knock the design against the round case a few times to loosen the butter. Refrigerate the butter mold until serving time.

To fill metal mold: Using the back of a metal spoon, press the butter firmly to fill each side of the mold. Bring both sides of the mold together to fit tightly. Refrigerate one hour, or freeze twenty minutes.

To unmold: With a sharp knife, carefully pry the metal mold open so that one side is freed from the butter. Gently pry the metal mold completely free from its other half. Refrigerate molded butter until serving time. (If the butter splits in half when the mold is opened, carefully pry out both sides of the butter; fit together; refrigerate.)

Note: Wooden molds become seasoned with use and easier to use. Plunger types of molds are available that make this process practically foolproof.

Butter Balls

Scald a pair of wooden butter paddles in boiling water to cover; then chill in ice water. Use one-and-one-half to two teaspoons firm butter or frozen margarine for each ball. Holding paddles parallel and at right angles to each other, rap the butter sharply between paddles. Then rotate paddles to form balls. Drop the balls into ice water; refrigerate, covered, until ready to use. Dip the paddles into ice water after making each ball, to keep them well chilled. A melon-ball scoop plunged first in hot water also performs this job well.

Butter Pats

Cut firm bar butter or frozen margarine into 1-inch-thick pats. Let stand at room temperature about ten minutes. With a sharp paring knife, make one-quarter-inch diagonal cuts at four corners of each pat. Gently turn each cut corner upward, to cup slightly. Place a parsley sprig in the center of each. Refrigerate until serving. You may also decorate them with miniature leaves or ferns and flowers.

Maple Butter

You may also flavor your butters. Make an old-fashioned maple butter by combining one-half cup soft butter, three tablespoons maple syrup, and one-quarter teaspoon maple extract. Beat with an electric mixer until it is light and fluffy. Refrigerate, covered, until time to use. Let stand at room temperature, to soften slightly, before serving. This will make about three-quarters of a cup.

Honey Butter

Prepare as for Maple Butter above, substituting honey for the maple syrup and vanilla extract for the maple extract.

Other Butters

Children enjoy cinnamon butter on their waffles. Simply blend a teaspoon of ground cinnamon and a tablespoon of powdered sugar into a stick of soft butter. Or add some finely chopped pecans or walnuts for a delicious butter to serve with any sweet bread. Sweetened, mashed berries may also be combined with butter if a bit of lemon juice is added. Or experiment with any of the various spices—nutmeg, coriander, ginger—you have on your shelf, adding confectioners' sugar to taste.

APRICOT SHORTBREAD

Shortbread

⅓ cup butter or margarine, softened

½ cup light-brown sugar, firmly packed

1 cup sifted all-purpose flour

Filling

¾ cup dried apricots

1 teaspoon grated lemon peel

⅔ cup granulated sugar

2 teaspoons cornstarch

⅓ cup chopped walnuts

1. Preheat oven to 350°F.
2. Make Shortbread: In medium-size bowl, with electric mixer, beat butter with brown sugar until light and fluffy.
3. At low speed, beat in flour.
4. Pat mixture evenly into bottom of an 8- by 8- by 2-inch baking pan. Bake 12 minutes, or until light golden in color. Let cool completely in pan on wire rack.
5. Meanwhile, make Filling: Place apricots in small saucepan. Add just enough water to cover; bring to boil. Reduce heat, and simmer, covered, 15 minutes. Drain apricots, reserving 3 tablespoons cooking liquid.
6. Chop apricots finely. Combine in small saucepan with reserved liquid, lemon peel, granulated sugar, and cornstarch. Bring to boil, stirring; boil 1 minute.
7. Let filling cool 10 minutes. Spread evenly over shortbread crust. Sprinkle with walnuts.
8. Bake 20 minutes. Let cool completely in pan on wire rack. Cut into bars.

Makes 20 bars.

BANANA BREAD

1¾ cups sifted all-purpose flour

⅔ cup sugar

3 teaspoons baking powder

½ teaspoon salt

¼ teaspoon baking soda
⅓ cup butter or margarine
1 cup mashed very ripe banana
(2 or 3)
2 eggs
½ cup chopped walnuts
¼ cup chopped candied citron

¼ cup chopped candied orange peel
¼ cup chopped candied cherries
¼ cup chopped candied pineapple
¼ cup dark seedless raisins

1. Preheat oven to 350°F. Grease well a 9- by 5- by 3-inch loaf pan.
2. Into large bowl, sift flour with sugar, baking powder, salt, and soda. With pastry blender, cut in butter until mixture resembles coarse crumbs.
3. Add banana and eggs; with electric mixer at low speed, beat 2 minutes.
4. Add nuts, candied fruit, and raisins; beat until well blended. Turn into prepared pan.
5. Bake 1 hour and 10 minutes, or until cake tester inserted in center comes out clean.
6. Let cool in pan on wire rack 10 minutes. Remove from pan; let cool completely on rack. Wrap with plastic film, then in foil, and store overnight before serving.

Makes 1 loaf.

BLUEBERRY OATMEAL BREAD

2 cups sifted all-purpose flour
1 teaspoon baking powder
1 teaspoon baking soda
1 teaspoon salt
½ teaspoon nutmeg or mace
1 cup raw quick-cooking oats
⅓ cup shortening, softened

½ cup light-brown sugar, firmly packed
2 eggs
1 cup buttermilk or sour milk*
1 cup chopped walnuts or pecans
1½ cups fresh or thawed frozen and drained blueberries

*To sour milk: Place 1½ teaspoons vinegar or lemon juice in a 1-cup measure. Add milk to measure 1 cup. Let stand a few minutes before using.

1. Preheat oven to 350°F. Grease well a 9- by 5- by 3-inch loaf pan.
2. Into large bowl, sift flour with baking powder, baking soda, salt, and nutmeg. Stir in oats.
3. In small bowl, using electric mixer at high speed, beat shortening, brown sugar, and eggs until smooth and fluffy. At low speed, beat in buttermilk.
4. Make a well in center of flour mixture. Pour in egg mixture; stir with fork just until dry ingredients are moistened and well blended.
5. Gently fold in nuts and blueberries just until combined.
6. Turn batter into prepared pan, spreading evenly.
7. Bake 60 minutes, or until cake tester inserted in center comes out clean.
8. Let cool in pan, on wire rack, 10 minutes. Turn out of pan; cool completely.
9. Wrap loaf in waxed paper or foil. Refrigerate overnight.
10. To serve: Cut into slices ½ inch thick.

Makes 1 loaf.

CHEESE BREAD

1 cup milk	1 teaspoon dry mustard
¼ cup sugar	⅛ teaspoon cayenne
1 tablespoon salt	4½ to 5 cups sifted all-purpose
½ cup warm water (105° to	flour
115°F.)	1 tablespoon butter or
2 packages active dry yeast	margarine, melted
¼ pound sharp Cheddar cheese, grated	

1. In small saucepan, heat milk just until bubbles form around edge of pan; remove from heat.
2. Add sugar and salt, stirring until dissolved; let cool to lukewarm.
3. If possible, check temperature of warm water with thermometer. Sprinkle yeast over water in large bowl, stirring until dissolved.
4. Stir in milk mixture, cheese, mustard, cayenne, and 2 cups flour. Beat with wooden spoon until smooth—about 2 minutes.

5. Gradually add remaining flour; mix in last of it with hand until dough leaves sides of bowl.

6. Turn dough onto lightly floured board. Knead until smooth—about 10 minutes.

7. Place in lightly greased large bowl. Brush top with melted butter. Cover with towel; let rise in warm place (85°F.), free from drafts, until double in bulk—about 2 hours.

8. Grease a 9- by 5- by 3-inch loaf pan.

9. Punch down dough; turn onto lightly floured pastry cloth. Shape dough into a smooth ball. Cover with towel; let rest 10 minutes.

10. Roll the ball into a 12- by 8-inch rectangle. From long side, roll up, jelly-roll fashion. Pinch edge, to seal. Place, seam side down, in prepared pan.

11. Cover the loaf with towel; let rise in warm place (85°F.), free from drafts, until double in bulk—about 1 hour.

12. Meanwhile, preheat oven to 400°F.

13. Bake loaf 20 minutes. Cover with foil, bake 10 to 15 minutes longer, or until loaf sounds hollow when rapped with knuckle.

14. Remove from pan to wire rack; cool completely.

Makes 1 loaf.

PEACH WALNUT BREAD

2 cups sifted all-purpose flour
½ cup sugar
3 teaspoons baking powder
1 teaspoon salt
½ teaspoon baking soda
1 cup snipped dried peaches

1 cup chopped walnuts
¼ cup salad oil
¾ cup milk
1 egg, beaten
1 teaspoon vanilla extract

1. Preheat oven to 350°F. Lightly grease a 9- by 5- by 3-inch loaf pan.

2. Into a large bowl, sift flour with sugar, baking powder, salt, and soda.

3. Add peaches and walnuts; mix well.

4. Add, in order: oil, milk, egg, and vanilla; stir with wooden spoon just until blended.

5. Turn into prepared pan; bake 45 to 50 minutes, or until a cake tester inserted in center comes out clean.

6. Let cool in pan, on wire rack, about 1 hour. Turn out of pan. To serve, slice thinly.

Makes about 12 slices.

APRICOT BRAN MUFFINS

1⅓ cups sifted all-purpose flour
1½ teaspoons baking powder
½ teaspoon baking soda
¼ teaspoon salt
2 cups whole-bran cereal
½ cup dried apricots, finely chopped; or ½ cup seedless raisins

⅓ cup butter or margarine, softened
½ cup light-brown sugar, firmly packed
2 tablespoons light molasses
1 egg
1 cup milk

1. Preheat oven to 400°F. Grease bottoms of 16 (2½-inch) muffin-pan cups.

2. Sift flour with baking powder, soda, and salt into medium-size bowl. Add bran cereal and apricots; mix well.

3. In large bowl, using wooden spoon, cream butter with brown sugar until light and fluffy. Beat in molasses and egg.

4. Add flour mixture, then milk, stirring with fork only until dry ingredients are moistened—do not beat. Batter will be lumpy. Spoon batter into prepared muffin-pan cups, filling two thirds full.

5. Bake 25 minutes, or until golden. Loosen edge of each muffin with spatula; turn out. Serve hot.

Makes 16 muffins.

BUTTERMILK BRAN MUFFINS

1 cup sifted all-purpose flour
2 teaspoons baking powder
¾ teaspoon salt
½ teaspoon baking soda
3 cups whole-bran cereal

½ cup seedless raisins
⅓ cup shortening
½ cup sugar
1 egg
1 cup buttermilk

1. Preheat oven to 400°F. Grease bottoms of 12 (3-inch) muffin-pan cups.

2. Into medium-size bowl, sift flour with baking powder, salt, and baking soda. Add whole-bran cereal and raisins; mix well.

3. In large bowl, using wooden spoon, cream shortening with sugar until light and fluffy. Beat in egg.

4. Add flour mixture alternately with buttermilk, stirring with fork only until dry ingredients are moistened. Do not beat. Batter will be lumpy. Quickly dip into prepared muffin pans, filling not quite two thirds full.

5. Bake 20 to 25 minutes, or until golden. Loosen edge of each muffin with spatula; turn out. Serve hot.

Makes 1 dozen muffins.

Note: If desired, make day before. Reheat, wrapped in foil, for breakfast.

HONEY BREAKFAST MUFFINS

1 cup sifted all-purpose flour	½ cup honey
2 teaspoons baking powder	½ cup coarsely chopped cooked
½ teaspoon salt	prunes
½ cup unsifted wholewheat	1 teaspoon grated orange peel
flour	¼ cup salad oil or melted
½ cup milk	shortening
1 egg, well beaten	

1. Preheat oven to 400°F., and lightly grease 9 (2½-inch) muffin-pan cups.

2. Into large bowl, sift the all-purpose flour with baking powder and salt.

3. Stir in wholewheat flour.

4. Combine milk and rest of ingredients in medium-size bowl. Add, all at once, to flour mixture, stirring only until mixture is moistened.

5. Spoon into cups; bake 20 to 25 minutes, or until nicely browned. Serve warm.

Makes 9 muffins.

BROWN-SUGAR BISCUITS WITH STERLING SAUCE

Sterling Sauce

⅓ cup butter or margarine, softened

⅔ cup light-brown sugar, firmly packed

1 teaspoon grated orange peel

1 tablespoon heavy cream

Brown-Sugar Biscuits

2 cups sifted all-purpose flour

¼ cup light-brown sugar, firmly packed

3 teaspoons baking powder

1 teaspoon salt

⅓ cup shortening, softened

⅔ to ¾ cup milk

1. Make Sterling Sauce: In small bowl, with electric mixer at medium speed, beat butter with ⅔ cup sugar until light.

2. Beat in orange peel and cream until well combined. Refrigerate, covered, until ready to use.

3. Preheat oven to 450°F.

4. Make Brown-Sugar Biscuits: Into large bowl, sift flour with ¼ cup sugar, baking powder, and salt.

5. Using pastry blender or 2 knives, cut in shortening until mixture resembles coarse cornmeal.

6. Make a well in center of dry ingredients. Pour in ⅔ cup milk all at once; stir quickly, with fork, until dry ingredients are moistened. Add a little more milk if flour mixture seems dry. Form dough into a ball.

7. On lightly floured surface, gently roll out dough ¾ inch thick. With floured, 2-inch biscuit cutter, cut straight down into dough, being careful not to twist cutter.

8. Place biscuits on lightly greased cookie sheet; bake 10 minutes, or until golden.

9. Remove to wire rack; cool slightly. Serve warm, with Sterling Sauce.

Makes 8 biscuits.

BLUEBERRY SCONES

2 cups sifted all-purpose flour
3 teaspoons baking powder
½ teaspoon salt
¼ cup sugar
⅓ cup salad oil

½ cup light cream
1 egg, unbeaten
1 cup fresh or thawed frozen
  and drained blueberries

1. Preheat oven to 425°F. Lightly grease a cookie sheet.
2. Into medium-size bowl, sift flour with baking powder, salt, and 2 tablespoons sugar.
3. Make a well in center of mixture. Add oil and cream, all at once. Add egg; stir with fork until well blended. Mixture will form a soft dough and clear sides of bowl.
4. With rubber scraper, gently fold in blueberries. Form dough into a ball.
5. Turn out dough onto a 12-inch square of waxed paper. Cover with another 12-inch square of waxed paper.
6. With rolling pin, roll the dough, between sheets of waxed paper, to form a 10-inch circle.
7. Peel off top sheet of waxed paper. Invert circle of dough on center of prepared cookie sheet. Peel off waxed paper.
8. Sprinkle surface evenly with remaining 2 tablespoons sugar.
9. Bake 20 minutes, or until golden brown. Remove to wire rack. Serve hot, cut into 12 pie-shape wedges.
Makes 12 scones.

IRISH BREAKFAST SCONES

3¼ cups packaged biscuit mix
5 tablespoons sugar
½ cup seedless raisins
1 cup milk

¼ teaspoon cinnamon
1 tablespoon butter or
  margarine, melted
1 tablespoon heavy cream

1. Preheat oven to 425°F.
2. In medium-size bowl, combine 3 cups biscuit mix, 2 tablespoons sugar, and the raisins; mix well.

3. With fork, stir in milk, to make a soft dough.

4. Turn out onto surface sprinkled with biscuit mix. Sprinkle dough with a little more biscuit mix, to keep the dough from sticking to the surface.

5. Roll out to ¾-inch thickness. Cut out rounds with floured 2½-inch biscuit cutter.

6. Arrange biscuits, 1 inch apart, on lightly greased cookie sheet; bake 15 minutes.

7. Meanwhile, combine remaining 3 tablespoons sugar with the cinnamon, butter, and cream, to make a paste.

8. Brush top of each scone with sugar mixture; bake 2 minutes longer, or until nicely browned.

Makes about 15 scones.

POPOVERS

3 eggs
1 cup milk
3 tablespoons salad oil

1 cup sifted all-purpose flour
½ teaspoon salt

1. Preheat oven to 400°F. Lightly grease 6 (5-ounce) custard cups and preheat them in the oven.

2. In medium-size bowl, with rotary beater, beat eggs, milk, and oil until well combined.

3. Sift flour with salt over egg mixture; beat just until smooth.

4. Pour batter into prepared custard cups, filling each about half full. Bake, on large cookie sheet, 45 to 50 minutes, or until deep golden brown. Do not open oven door while they are baking. Serve hot.

Makes 6 popovers.

COCOA BREAKFAST CRESCENTS

2 tablespoons butter or
  margarine
2 tablespoons sugar
1 tablespoon cocoa
3 tablespoons chopped walnuts

1 package (8 ounces)
  refrigerated crescent dinner
  rolls

Confectioners' sugar
Butter

1. Preheat oven to 375°F.

2. In small bowl, cream butter with sugar until smooth; stir in cocoa and nuts.

3. Unroll dough from package; separate into triangles. Place about 1 teaspoon cocoa mixture on each triangle; spread mixture to ½ inch from edges. Roll up each, starting at wide end. Place rolls, point side down, 1 inch apart, on ungreased cookie sheet; curve, to make crescents.

4. Bake 10 to 13 minutes, or until golden brown.

5. Let cool on cookie sheet on wire rack 5 minutes. Sprinkle with confectioners' sugar. Serve warm, with butter.

Makes 8 crescents.

POPPY-SEED CRESCENTS AND SESAME-SEED ROLLS

1 package (8 ounces) refrigerated crescent dinner rolls

1 package (8.6 ounces) refrigerated butterflake dinner rolls

1 egg
Poppy seeds
Sesame seeds

1. Preheat oven to 375°F. Shape crescent-roll dough, and place on cookie sheet, as package label directs. Separate butterflake rolls, and place in muffin cups, as package label directs for 6 rolls.

2. In a small bowl, beat egg with a fork. Brush lightly on tops of rolls. Sprinkle crescents with poppy seeds, butterflake rolls with sesame seeds.

3. Bake as package labels direct, or until golden brown.

4. Arrange in napkin-lined basket. Serve warm.

Makes 14 rolls.

SALT CRESCENTS

2 packages (8-ounce size) refrigerated crescent dinner rolls

1 egg, slightly beaten
2 teaspoons coarse salt

1. Preheat oven to 375°F.
2. Shape crescents, and place on cookie sheet, as package label directs.
3. Brush crescents with egg; sprinkle with salt.
4. Bake 12 minutes, or until golden brown.
Makes 16 crescents.

SUNDAY-BREAKFAST CRESCENTS

5 tablespoons butter or margarine
½ cup pineapple preserves
½ cup flaked coconut

2 packages (8-ounce size) refrigerated crescent dinner rolls

Confectioners' sugar

1. Preheat oven to 375°F.
2. In small bowl, beat 4 tablespoons butter with the pineapple preserves until well blended. Stir in coconut.
3. Unroll dough, and separate into triangles. Place about 1 tablespoon preserves mixture on wide end of each triangle. Roll up, starting at wide end and rolling to point.
4. Place rolls, point side down and just touching, in 2 rows in buttered 9- by 9- by 2-inch baking pan.
5. Melt remaining tablespoon butter. Brush over rolls.
6. Bake about 30 minutes, or until golden brown.
7. Cool in pan on wire rack about 5 minutes. Turn out of pan; turn right side up onto serving plate. Sprinkle with sugar. Serve warm.
Makes 8 servings, 16 rolls.

CARAMEL-PECAN ROLLS

2 tablespoons butter or margarine
½ cup light-brown sugar, firmly packed

2 tablespoons light corn syrup
18 pecan halves
1 package (9.3 ounces) refrigerator butterflake rolls

1. Preheat oven to 375°F.

2. Melt butter in small saucepan. Remove from heat.

3. Add sugar and corn syrup; cook, over low heat, stirring, until sugar dissolves.

4. Divide syrup mixture into bottoms of 6 (2½-inch) muffin-pan cups. Arrange 3 pecan halves over syrup in each cup.

5. For each roll, stand 3 pieces of dough, on edge, in each muffin-pan cup.

6. Place foil under pan, to catch any runover. Bake 20 minutes, or until golden brown.

7. Let cool in pan 5 minutes. Invert onto serving plate. Replace nuts. Makes 6 rolls.

ONION ROLLS

1   cup milk
2   tablespoons sugar
1   teaspoon salt
Dash pepper
¼   cup butter or margarine

¼   cup warm water (105° to 115°F.)
1   package active dry yeast
4   cups sifted all-purpose flour

Topping

4   medium onions
¼   cup butter or margarine
1   egg, beaten

¼   cup dairy sour cream
½   teaspoon salt
1   tablespoon poppy seed

1. In small saucepan, heat milk just until bubbles form around edge of pan.

2. Remove from heat. Add sugar, salt, pepper, and butter; stir until butter is melted. Let cool to lukewarm.

3. If possible, check temperature of warm water with thermometer. Sprinkle yeast over water in large bowl, stirring until dissolved. Stir in milk mixture.

4. Add 2½ cups flour. With wooden spoon, beat until smooth—about 2 minutes.

5. Add remaining flour; mix in last of it with hand until dough leaves sides of bowl.

6. Cover with damp towel. Let rise in warm place (85°F.), free from drafts, about 1 hour, or until double in bulk.

7. Meanwhile, make Topping: Peel onions; slice very thinly. (Onion will measure about 1½ cups.)

8. In hot butter in medium-size skillet, sauté onion, stirring occasionally, about 10 minutes, or until it is tender. Let cool.

9. In small bowl, combine egg, sour cream, and salt; mix well. Also, grease 2 large cookie sheets.

10. Turn out dough onto lightly floured pastry cloth. Knead until smooth.

11. Shape dough into a roll, 12 inches long. Cut crosswise into 12 pieces. Shape each piece into a ball.

12. Place balls, 3 inches apart, on prepared cookie sheets. Flatten each with palm of hand to a circle, 3 inches in diameter.

13. Press onion slices into circles of dough. Spread with sour-cream mixture; then sprinkle with poppy seed.

14. Let rise in warm place (85°F.), free from drafts, until double in bulk—about 1 hour.

15. Meanwhile, preheat oven to 375°F. Bake rolls 20 to 25 minutes, or until golden brown. Serve warm.

Makes 12 rolls.

GOLDEN SQUASH ROLLS

⅔ cup milk
1 package (12 ounces) frozen cooked squash, thawed; or 1 cup cooked squash
⅓ cup light-brown sugar, firmly packed
¾ teaspoon salt

2½ tablespoons butter or margarine
¼ cup lukewarm water (105° to 115°F.)
1 package active dry yeast
4 to 5 cups sifted all-purpose flour
Butter or margarine, melted

1. In small saucepan, heat milk just until bubbles form around edge.

2. In large, warm mixing bowl, combine milk, squash, sugar, salt, and 2½ tablespoons butter; stir to mix well.

3. If possible, check temperature of water with thermometer. In small bowl, pour water over yeast; stir to dissolve yeast.

4. Add yeast and 2 cups flour to squash mixture. Beat vigorously, with wooden spoon, until smooth—about 2 minutes.

5. Gradually beat in 2 cups of remaining flour. If necessary, beat in more flour to make dough stiff enough to clear sides of bowl and handle easily.

6. Turn out dough onto lightly floured surface. Let rest, covered, 5 minutes. Knead until smooth and elastic—for about 5 minutes—adding more flour to surface as needed.

7. Place dough in large, greased bowl. Lightly brush with melted butter. Cover with sheet of waxed paper, then with dish towel.

8. Let rise in warm place (85°F.), free from drafts, until double in bulk—about 1½ hours. (Finger inserted in dough will make a hole.)

9. Punch down dough. Turn out on lightly floured surface. To shape like Parker House rolls: Roll out dough ⅜ inch thick. Cut with 2½-inch biscuit cutter. Make crease, slightly off-center, with dull edge of knife. Brush lightly with a little melted butter. Fold over smaller part; press folded edge.

10. Place rolls, about 1½ inches apart, on greased cookie sheets. Cover with waxed paper; let rise in warm place until double in bulk—about 1 hour. (Fingertip will leave an imprint in roll.) Meanwhile, preheat oven to 400°F.

11. Brush rolls lightly with melted butter. Bake about 20 minutes, or until golden. Serve hot.

Makes about 2½ dozen rolls.

SWEET-ROLL DOUGH

¾ cup milk
½ cup sugar
2 teaspoons salt
½ cup butter or margarine
½ cup warm water (105° to 115°F.)

2 packages active dry yeast
2 eggs, beaten
4¼ cups unsifted all-purpose flour
Butter or margarine, softened

1. Heat the milk just until bubbles form. Add sugar, salt, and ½ cup butter; stir to dissolve. Cool to lukewarm.

2. If possible, check temperature of warm water with thermometer. Pour into large, warm bowl. Sprinkle the yeast over water, and stir to dissolve.

3. With a wooden spoon, stir in milk mixture, beaten eggs, and 2 cups flour; beat until smooth—about 2 minutes.

4. Gradually add rest of the flour, beating until dough is stiff, smooth, and clears sides of bowl. Turn into large, greased bowl. Brush with softened butter.

5. Cover the bowl with foil; refrigerate for 2 hours. Dough will rise to top. (May be refrigerated up to 3 days.)

6. To use: Cut off amount needed; refrigerate the remainder. Shape and bake as directed.

Makes 2 dozen rolls.

ORANGE STICKY BUNS

Orange Glaze

¼ cup light corn syrup
1½ tablespoons grated orange peel
3 tablespoons orange juice
2 tablespoons butter or margarine
⅓ cup coarsely chopped walnuts

⅓ recipe Sweet-Roll Dough (see p. 194)
2 tablespoons butter or margarine, softened
About ¼ cup bottled cinnamon sugar
¼ cup dark seedless raisins

1. Lightly grease an 8- by 8- by 2-inch baking pan.

2. Make Orange Glaze: In small saucepan, over medium heat, bring syrup, orange peel, orange juice, and 2 tablespoons butter to boiling. Reduce heat; simmer, uncovered, 5 minutes, or until slightly thickened.

3. Reserve 2 tablespoons glaze for later. Pour rest of glaze into prepared pan. Sprinkle nuts on glaze.

4. Make Sweet-Roll Dough.

5. On lightly floured surface, shape dough into a round; let rest 5 minutes.

6. Roll dough into an 18- by 9-inch rectangle. Spread with softened butter; then sprinkle with cinnamon sugar and raisins.

7. From long side, roll up dough tightly, jelly-roll fashion. With sharp knife, cut crosswise to make 16 (1⅛-inch-thick) pieces.

8. Arrange, cut side down, evenly spaced, in the glaze in pan. Brush the tops with the reserved glaze. Cover loosely with a sheet of waxed paper.

9. Let rise in warm place (85°F.), free from drafts, until double in bulk—about 45 minutes. Meanwhile, preheat oven to 375°F.

10. Bake 25 to 30 minutes, or until buns are golden brown and syrup has thickened.

11. Place sheet of waxed paper on wire rack. Invert pan of hot buns on paper. If any glaze remains in pan, spread on buns with spatula. Let cool on wire rack.

Makes 16 buns.

SCHNECKEN

Filling

1 package (4½ ounces) almond macaroons, crushed	2 packages (8-ounce size) refrigerator crescent rolls
½ cup butter or margarine, melted	3 tablespoons finely chopped almonds
2 tablespoons sugar	3 tablespoons sugar
½ teaspoon almond extract	1 egg white

1. Preheat oven to 375°F.

2. Make Filling: In small bowl, combine macaroons, butter, 2 tablespoons sugar, extract; mix well.

3. Unroll crescent-roll dough from both packages. Cut along perforations, to make 16 pieces of dough. Spread each with a slightly rounded tablespoon of filling; roll up as package label directs; press end gently, to seal. Place on ungreased cookie sheet.

4. Mix almonds with sugar. Beat egg white with 1 tablespoon water; brush over rolls. Sprinkle with almond mixture.

5. Bake 15 minutes, or until golden brown. Serve warm.

Makes 16 schnecken.

KIFLI

Dough

4 cups unsifted all-purpose flour

2 cups butter or margarine

4 egg yolks, slightly beaten

1 cup dairy sour cream

Filling

1¼ pounds walnuts, ground

1 cup granulated sugar

½ cup milk

1 tablespoon almond extract

1 egg, beaten

Confectioners' sugar

1. Make Dough: Place flour in large bowl. With pastry blender, cut in butter until mixture resembles coarse crumbs. Add egg yolks and sour cream; stir until combined. Turn out on lightly floured surface, and knead until dough is smooth and can be shaped into a ball. If too sticky, knead in more flour. (Dough can be refrigerated until ready to use.)

2. Make Filling: In medium-size bowl, combine nuts, granulated sugar, milk, and almond extract; blend well.

3. Preheat oven to 400°F. Grease cookie sheets.

4. To shape kifli: On lightly floured surface, roll out one quarter of dough at a time, to measure 16 by 12 inches, ⅛ inch thick. With pastry wheel, cut into 2-inch squares.

5. Place a generous ½ teaspoon filling in the center of each square; then bring 2 opposite corners, overlapping, over filling; pinch corners together, to seal. Place on cookie sheets. Brush lightly with egg.

6. Bake 12 minutes, or until golden. Remove, and roll in confectioners' sugar. Let cool on wire rack.

Makes 16 dozen kifli.

PECAN COFFEECAKE

1⅓ cups packaged biscuit mix

¾ cup granulated sugar

¾ cup milk

1 egg

3 tablespoons butter or margarine, softened

1 teaspoon vanilla extract

Topping

½ cup light-brown sugar, firmly
packed

½ cup pecan halves

¼ cup butter or margarine,
softened

2 tablespoons light cream or
undiluted evaporated milk

1. Preheat oven to 350°F. Grease and flour an 8- by 8- by 2-inch baking dish.

2. In small bowl of electric mixer, combine biscuit mix, sugar, ¼ cup milk, the egg, 3 tablespoons butter, and the vanilla; beat at medium speed 1 minute, or just until smooth. Add remaining milk; beat ½ minute. Turn batter into prepared baking dish.

3. Bake 35 to 40 minutes, or until cake tester inserted in center comes out clean.

4. Meanwhile, make Topping: Combine all topping ingredients in small bowl; mix well.

5. Spread topping evenly over baked coffeecake. Run under broiler, 4 inches from heat, 2 to 3 minutes, or until topping is bubbly and golden brown. Serve warm, cut into 9 squares.

Makes 9 servings.

PRUNE-AND-APRICOT COFFEECAKE

¾ cup dried prunes

¾ cup dried apricots

⅔ cup light-brown sugar, firmly
packed

1 tablespoon flour

1 tablespoon cinnamon

2 cups unsifted all-purpose
flour

2 teaspoons baking powder

½ teaspoon salt

¾ cup shortening, softened

¾ cup granulated sugar

2 eggs

1 teaspoon vanilla extract

¾ cup milk

6 tablespoons butter or
margarine, melted

⅓ cup chopped walnuts

1. Let prunes and apricots stand in hot water, to cover, 5 minutes. Drain fruit, and chop finely. Set aside.

2. Preheat oven to 350°F. Lightly grease and flour a 9-inch tube pan. In small bowl, combine brown sugar, 1 tablespoon flour, and the cinnamon. Set aside. Sift 2 cups flour with baking powder and salt. Set aside.

3. In large bowl, with electric mixer at high speed, beat shortening, granulated sugar, eggs, and vanilla till light and fluffy—about 5 minutes.

4. At low speed, beat in flour mixture (in thirds) alternately with milk (in halves), beginning and ending with flour mixture; beat just until combined.

5. With rubber scraper, gently fold in prunes and apricots.

6. Turn one third of batter into prepared pan, spreading evenly. Sprinkle with one third of brown-sugar mixture, then with 2 tablespoons melted butter. Repeat layering twice. Sprinkle top with walnuts.

7. Bake 55 minutes, or until cake tester inserted near center comes out clean. Let cool in pan on wire rack about 25 minutes. Remove from pan, and serve warm.

Makes 8 servings.

To do ahead: Before guests arrive, prepare cake as directed in Steps 1 through 6. Refrigerate in pan, covered. Then, just before serving, bake, and cool slightly.

APPLE-APRICOT KUCHEN

1 cup dried apricot halves	2 medium cooking apples (1 to
2 cups sifted all-purpose flour	1¼ pounds)
1 cup sugar	1 teaspoon cinnamon
¼ teaspoon salt	3 egg yolks
½ cup butter or margarine	1½ cups heavy cream

1. In small saucepan, combine apricots and 1 cup water; bring to boil. Remove from heat; cover; let stand 30 minutes, to soften.

2. In medium-size bowl, combine flour, 2 tablespoons sugar, and the salt. With pastry blender, cut in butter until the mixture resembles coarse crumbs.

3. Turn mixture into a 10-inch springform pan, and pat firmly on bottom and about 1½ inches up the sides.

4. Quarter, peel, and core apples. Cut into about ⅓ -inch-thick slices. Drain apricots.

5. Preheat oven to 400°F.

6. Arrange some of apple slices and apricot halves, alternately and overlapping, around edge of pastry-lined pan. Arrange remaining fruit in center. Combine remaining sugar with the cinnamon. Sprinkle over fruit. Bake 15 minutes.

7. Beat egg yolks with cream. Pour over fruit. Bake 30 to 35 minutes longer, or until egg mixture has set and top is golden brown.

8. Let cool 10 minutes. Gently release spring, and remove the side of the pan. Serve kuchen warm, cut in wedges.

Makes 1 (10-inch) kuchen.

COFFEE KUCHEN

3 cups sifted all-purpose flour	3 tablespoons instant coffee
3 teaspoons baking powder	½ cup butter or margarine
¼ teaspoon salt	½ cup shortening
1¼ teaspoons cinnamon	1 cup milk
1 cup granulated sugar	⅛ teaspoon baking soda
1 cup light-brown sugar, firmly packed	2 eggs, slightly beaten

1. Preheat oven to 350°F. Lightly grease and flour a 9-inch tube pan.

2. Into large bowl, sift flour with baking powder, salt, cinnamon, sugars, and coffee.

3. Using pastry blender or 2 knives, cut butter and shortening into flour mixture until mixture resembles small peas. Set aside 1 cup mixture for topping.

4. Combine milk with baking soda and eggs; mix well. With wooden spoon, stir all at once into flour mixture just until combined.

5. Turn into tube pan. Sprinkle evenly with the reserved topping mixture.

6. Bake 55 to 60 minutes, or until cake tester inserted in center comes out clean.

7. Let cool, in pan, on wire rack 10 minutes. Remove from pan; serve warm.

Makes 10 servings.

PINEAPPLE-APRICOT-NUT LOAF

2¾ cups sifted all-purpose flour
3 teaspoons baking powder
¼ teaspoon baking soda
¼ teaspoon salt
¾ cup sugar
⅓ cup butter, melted
1 egg
⅓ cup milk

1 cup canned crushed
  pineapple, undrained
⅓ cup chopped dried apricots
¼ cup light seedless raisins
1 tablespoon chopped candied
  green cherries or citron
1 cup chopped walnuts

1. Preheat oven to 350°F. Grease and flour a 9- by 5- by 3-inch loaf pan. Sift flour with baking powder, soda, and salt; set aside.

2. In large bowl, combine sugar, melted butter, and egg; using wooden spoon, beat until ingredients are well blended.

3. Add milk, pineapple, apricots, raisins, and cherries; blend well.

4. Add flour mixture; beat just until combined. Stir in nuts. Turn into prepared pan.

5. Bake 1¼ hours, or until cake tester inserted in center comes out clean.

6. Let cool in the pan 10 minutes. Remove from pan; let cool completely on wire rack.

Makes 1 loaf.

LEMON POUNDCAKE

1 package (8 ounces) cream
  cheese, softened
4 eggs
1 package (1 pound, 2½
  ounces) yellow-cake mix

¾ cup milk
2 tablespoons grated lemon
  peel

Confectioners' sugar (optional)

1. Preheat oven to 350°F. Grease well and flour a 9-inch tube pan.

2. In large bowl of electric mixer, at medium speed, beat cheese until light and fluffy. Scrape beaters with rubber scraper.

3. Add eggs, one at a time, beating well after each addition.

4. At low speed, beat in cake mix (in 3 additions) alternately with milk (in 2 additions), beginning and ending with cake mix; beat just until well combined. Blend in lemon peel.

5. Turn into prepared pan; bake 55 minutes, or until cake tester inserted in center comes out clean.

6. Let cake stand in pan on wire rack 15 minutes; then turn out onto wire rack; cool completely. If desired, sprinkle with confectioners' sugar.

Makes 12 servings.

Note: This cake is better if made the day before. Store, wrapped in foil, in refrigerator.

GINGER POUNDCAKE

3 cups sifted all-purpose flour	1 cup butter or margarine, softened
½ teaspoon baking powder	½ cup light-brown sugar, firmly packed
½ teaspoon baking soda	
½ teaspoon salt	½ cup granulated sugar
1 teaspoon cinnamon	3 eggs
1 teaspoon ginger	½ cup milk
¼ teaspoon allspice	1 cup light molasses
¼ teaspoon nutmeg	

1. Preheat oven to 325°F. Grease well and flour a 3-quart bundt mold or a 9-inch tube pan.

2. Sift flour with baking powder, soda, salt, and spices; set aside.

3. In large bowl of electric mixer, at medium speed, beat butter and sugars until light and fluffy.

4. Add eggs, one at a time, beating after each addition. Continue beating until mixture is very light and fluffy.

5. Combine milk and molasses, mixing very well.

6. At low speed, beat in flour mixture (in fourths) alternately with milk-molasses mixture (in thirds), beginning and ending with flour mixture. Beat just until batter is smooth and well combined.

7. Turn batter into prepared pan; bake about 1 hour and 10 minutes, or until cake tester inserted in center comes out clean.

8. Cool in pan, on wire rack, 15 minutes. Turn out of pan onto wire rack; cool completely.

9. Serve thinly sliced.

Makes 16 servings.

SAFFRON-CURRANT POUNDCAKE

2 packages (1-pound, 1-ounce size) poundcake mix	1½ cups milk
¾ cup dried currants	4 eggs
Pinch saffron threads, crumbled	Confectioners' sugar

1. Preheat oven to 325°F. Grease well and flour a 10-inch kugelhopf mold or tube pan.

2. In large bowl of electric mixer, combine cake mix and currants.

3. Dissolve saffron in the milk. Add 1 cup milk mixture to cake mix and currants; beat, at low speed, 1 minute, scraping sides of bowl with rubber scraper.

4. Add eggs; beat, at low speed, 1½ minutes.

5. Add rest of milk mixture; beat 1 minute longer.

6. Pour batter into prepared pan; bake 1 hour and 35 minutes, or until cake tester inserted in center comes out clean.

7. Let cake stand in pan 10 minutes. Run a small spatula around sides of cake to loosen; then turn out onto wire rack. Let cake cool completely.

8. Before serving, sprinkle confectioners' sugar over top of cake. Cut into thin slices.

Makes 16 servings.

SPONGE CAKE

6   eggs (1⅓ cups)   1½   teaspoons vanilla extract
1   cup warm milk
2   cups sifted all-purpose flour   Confectioners' sugar
2   teaspoons baking powder
½   teaspoon salt   Frosting (optional)
2   cups granulated sugar

1. In large bowl of electric mixer, let eggs warm to room temperature—about 1 hour.

2. In small saucepan, heat milk just until bubbles form around edge of pan. Remove from heat; set aside.

3. Preheat oven to 350°F. Sift flour with baking powder and salt; set aside.

4. At high speed, beat eggs until thick and lemon-colored—3 or 4 minutes. Gradually add granulated sugar, beating until mixture is very thick—about 5 minutes.

5. At low speed, blend in flour mixture just until smooth.

6. Add warm milk and the vanilla, beating just until combined.

7. Pour batter immediately into an ungreased 13- by 9- by 2-inch baking pan. Bake 35 to 40 minutes, or until surface springs back when gently pressed with fingertip.

8. Let cake hang upside down between 2 other pans; let cool completely. Gently remove from pan.

9. Serve lightly sprinkled with confectioners' sugar, or frost as desired. Cut into 12 squares.

Makes 12 servings.

MARBLE SPONGE CAKE

Sponge Cake batter (see above)   Chocolate Glaze (see p. 205)
¼   cup sifted, unsweetened
    cocoa

1. Make Sponge Cake batter, reducing flour to 1¾ cups.
2. Divide batter in half. Fold cocoa into one half of the batter.
3. Into an ungreased 10-inch tube pan, pour plain batter alternately with cocoa batter. Bake 45 to 50 minutes, or until a cake tester inserted in center comes out clean.
4. Invert pan over neck of bottle; let cake cool completely. Glaze with Chocolate Glaze.

Makes 12 servings.

CHOCOLATE GLAZE

1 package (6 ounces) semisweet-chocolate pieces

2 tablespoons butter or margarine
2 tablespoons light corn syrup

1. In top part of double boiler, over hot, not boiling, water, melt chocolate with butter, corn syrup, and 2 tablespoons hot water.
2. Stir to blend well.
3. With spatula, spread over top of Marble Sponge Cake, letting some run down side of cake.
4. Let cake stand about 1 hour, or until glaze is firm enough to cut.

Makes about ¾ cup.

9

MENUS

Planter's Punch
Shrimp-and-Crab-Meat Scrambled Eggs
Glazed Canadian Bacon
Schnecken
Coffee

Use your imagination to put together this cold weather brunch. Set out the icy but invigorating punch in a heavy pewter punch bowl before ladling it into prechilled ceramic coconut shells or mugs. The Shrimp-and-Crab-Meat Scrambled Eggs, with its own Newburg Sauce, might be served directly from an attractive skillet made of bright enamelware. Carve a few slices from the Glazed Canadian Bacon and arrange them, along with orange slices and spiced crabapples, around the whole bacon set on a white ceramic platter. Top off your brunch with tiny Schnecken, and pour out cups of freshly perked coffee.

Rosé-Wine Spritzer
Sherried Fruit Cup
Breast of Turkey Chaud-Froid
Marinated Asparagus/ Savory Stuffed Mushrooms
Poppy-Seed Crescents and Sesame-Seed Rolls
Ginger Poundcake with Lime Sherbet
Coffee

For a buffet brunch, serve Breast of Turkey Chaud-Froid as a main dish. Set your buffet table with a white cloth and use accessories in bright colors for contrast. Several small bowls of fruit make pretty centerpieces—for instance, green grapes, strawberries, lemons or limes, peaches, and purple grapes. Bring out your bowl of Rosé-Wine Spritzer to accompany the meal. Set out another glass bowl containing layers of Sherried Fruit Cup, to be scooped out later into chilled sherbet glasses. Place the glazed and garnished turkey in the center of the table. Serve side dishes of Marinated Asparagus and Savory Stuffed Mushrooms (prepare both the day before and bake the mushrooms just before the guests sit down to eat), and pass warm Poppy-Seed Crescents and Sesame-Seed Rolls. To end this meal, serve scoops of lime sherbet alongside slices of spicy Ginger Poundcake.

Pineapple Swizzles
French Omelet with Chicken Livers
Buttermilk Bran Muffins
Conserves and Jams
Coffee

For a pleasant change from the normal Sunday family breakfast fare, serve a golden-brown French omelet filled with sautéed chicken livers and bacon (see page 62). Whet the family's appetites with tangy Pineapple Swizzles garnished with maraschino cherries, mint sprigs, and pineapple chunks. Or, if you are serving from a punch bowl, float orange and lime slices on top. Serve a tray of freshly made Buttermilk

Bran Muffins, laced with raisins, and offer a variety of conserves. Pour cups of coffee to end the meal.

Champagne Punch Bowl
French Onion Soup
Salmon Soufflé with Oyster Sauce
Golden Squash Rolls
Pineapple au Naturel
Coffee

For a midwinter brunch, perhaps one for guests from out of town, serve this menu, which is perfectly suited to a somewhat formal meal. Begin with a refreshing Champagne Punch Bowl, garnished with grapes and strawberries. The steaming French Onion Soup, topped with thick slices of toasted French bread, could be ladled from a handsome tureen into painted china soup bowls. Serve the Salmon Soufflé onto attractive plates, and pour the creamy Oyster Sauce over each helping. Pass the plate of delicately flavored Golden Squash Rolls. End with Pineapple au Naturel, piled high into chilled sherbet dishes, and mugs of hot coffee.

Margaritas
Tossed Green Salad Bowl
Swiss Fondue
French Bread
Fresh-Fruit Extravaganza
Espresso

For an imaginative brunch, give a fondue party (see page 79). This is a perfect meal to serve during the first football game of the season on television. Guests should be able to reach everything comfortably without inconveniencing themselves. Use a coffee table, set with gay straw placemats, sectioned enameled fondue plates, long-handled fondue forks, and wooden salad bowls. Set the Tossed Green Salad Bowl on the table, and let the guests help themselves. Tear the French bread into chunks that can be speared and dipped into the fondue bubbling away in the enameled fondue pot or copper chafing dish. Ladle out the Margaritas—throughout the meal unless you prefer to serve them before the meal and offer a white wine with the brunch. When the table has been cleared for the Espresso, bring in the chilled Fresh-Fruit Extravaganza and set it in the center of your table, again so that each guest can help himself to the delicious array before him.

Frosty Daiquiri Punch with Fern Ice Block
Sweetbreads in White Wine in Patty Shells
Marinated Vegetable Salad Platter
Honeydew-and-Green-Grape Fantasy
Coffee

Delectable Sweetbreads in White Wine form the basis of a lovely summer brunch—perfect for a bridge party or a meeting of the ladies' auxiliary. The day before your brunch, prepare the frosted punch bowl and the Fern Ice Block. Marinate the vegetables for your Marinated Vegetable Salad Platter—green beans, whole beets, asparagus, carrots, tomatoes, and artichokes. Prepare the Frosty Daiquiri Punch at least three hours before your guests arrive and allow it to chill. While your guests are drinking their punch, prepare a plate of the baked patty shells and sweetbreads for each person. Follow the main course with a decorative arrangement of Honeydew-and-Green-Grape Fantasy and freshly brewed coffee.

Bloody Marys
Cantaloupe Balls à l'Orange
Omelets Made to Order
Prune-and-Apricot Coffeecake
Coffee

For a family gathering, offer a selection of omelets made to order (see page 64). One of the various fillings—red caviar and sour cream, creamed oyster, creamed spinach, muenster cheese with caraway, or chicken liver and mushrooms—is bound to satisfy each taste. (An eight-inch omelet pan is a help here.) Begin by bringing in a pitcher of Bloody Marys, preparing a second pitcher without vodka for the children. When all are seated, bring each person a dish of Cantaloupe

Balls marinated in orange juice and kirsch, then garnished with mint. After the omelets serve a luscious homemade Prune-and-Apricot Coffeecake and a pot of coffee.

Sangría

Cold Lobster with Herb Hollandaise Sauce

Peach-Currant Salad Mold

Lemon Poundcake

Coffee

On a scorching summer day, plan your brunch for the patio or garden. Serve Cold Lobster with Herb Hollandaise Sauce accompanied by a pretty Peach-Currant Salad unmolded on crisp salad greens—both can be prepared the day before your gathering. Before bringing out the frosty pitchers of red-wine Sangría, set the table—or several card tables—with a white linen cloth, and arrange a centerpiece of freshly cut flowers. Follow the main course of this light summer meal with wedges of airy Lemon Poundcake and coffee, iced if you prefer.

Breakfast Orange Blossoms

Fresh Grapefruit Halves with Orange Sections

Surprise Pancakes

Baked Eggs Gruyère

Baked Ham, Sausage, and Bacon

Coffee/Milk

If you are planning a brunch for a special family occasion, children included, try serving Surprise Pancakes, made with raisins and wheat germ, with hot maple syrup. Baked Eggs Gruyère is the main course. Accompany them with a platter of Baked Ham, Sausage, and Bacon. You may wish to bake a whole ham for the occasion, or simply serve slices of store-bought ham. Breakfast Orange Blossoms are both refreshing and nutritious, and Fresh Grapefruit Halves with Orange Sections will offer a contrast to the sweetness of the pancakes to come. Hot coffee and milk for the children complete this hearty meal.

Piña Coladas
Gazpacho Andaluz
Chicken Livers en Brochette on Rice
Harvest Fruit Bowl
Sponge Cake
Coffee

Begin this lively brunch with an exotic punch prepared from pineapple juice and cream of coconut mixed with a generous amount of light rum (see page 20). To whet the appetite, serve a soup course first—refreshing Gazpacho Andaluz, premixed in your blender and garnished with all the accompaniments at the table, looks lovely served in sherbet glasses. Chicken Livers broiled on a skewer with fresh whole mushrooms and slices of bacon interspersed provide the main course (see·page 118). Following directions given on the package, prepare enough rice to serve as beds for the brochettes. Follow with a Harvest Fruit Bowl containing orange and grapefruit sections, apple and pear wedges, grapes laced with marsala, and pitted dates. Accompany with Sponge Cake and hot coffee.

Hot Mulled Cider
English Mixed Grill
French-Fried Potatoes
Popovers
Fresh-Fruit Melon-Go-Round
Irish Coffee

Whether or not you can offer the ambience of an oak-paneled dining room, this British club-style brunch will please even the heartiest eater. Because it has been designed for chilly days, the menu begins with a spicy Hot Mulled Cider, redolent with cloves and cinnamon. A broiled English Mixed Grill follows, featuring a variety of choice meats— sausages, bacon slices, lamb chops, and rump steaks. Crisp French-Fried Potatoes might accompany it, as well as Popovers. Finish with mugs of Irish Coffee (or regular coffee if you prefer) and a platter laden with wedges of honeydew or Spanish melon and garnished with whole, unpeeled, perfect nectarines or peaches, purple grapes, and sprigs of fresh mint (see page 37).

Fruit Punch
Poached Plums Cardamom
Curried-Chicken-Salad Mold
Peach Walnut Bread
Coffee

A cold Curried-Chicken-Salad Mold, prettily garnished with pimiento-stuffed olives and sprigs of crisp watercress, is the basis of this delightful brunch, perfectly suited to a midsummer garden or patio setting. Precede the molded salad with tumblers of refreshing Fruit Punch and bowlfuls of fragrant Poached Plums Cardamom. Peach Walnut Bread and hot coffee provide a gracious end to a superb meal.

Champagne Punch Bowl
Baked Striped Bass / Trout Amandine
Spinach Soufflé
Baked Tomato Halves
Cheese Bread
Strawberries Romanoff
Coffee

Delicious fresh fish forms the basis of this elegant brunch. Start with a Champagne Punch Bowl, impressive as well as refreshing, combining champagne with sauterne and soda. Follow with the whole bass or trout (see pages 134 and 159)—preferably fresh-caught. Either makes a spectacular dish. A Spinach Soufflé and Baked Tomato Halves with crumbed tops make fine accompaniments to your main dish. Homemade Cheese Bread, baked the day before and served at room temperature, is delicious with this meal. And the perfect ending is Strawberries Romanoff—fresh berries folded into sweetened heavy cream and seasoned with a splash of cointreau.

Index

Index

Brown-sugar biscuits with sterling sauce, 187
Brunches, general data on, 1-4
Brussels sprouts, general data on, 163
Buns, orange sticky, 195-196
Butter, 178-180
  balls, 179-180
  cinnamon, 180
  curls, 178-179
  honey, 180
  -lemon-chive sauce, scallops with, 152
  maple, 180
Buttermilk
  bran muffins, 185-186
  pancakes with strawberries and sour cream, 80-81

Café brûlot, 17-18
Caffè espresso, 7
Cakes
  coffeecake
    apple-apricot kuchen, 199-200
    coffee kuchen, 200-201
    pecan, 197-198
    prune and apricot, 198-199
  pineapple-apricot-nut loaf, 201
  poundcake
    ginger, 202-203
    lemon, 201-202
    saffron-currant, 203
  sponge, 204
    marble, 204-205
Canadian bacon
  bananas and, 103
  glazed, 104
Cantaloupe
  general data on, 29
  melon ball coupe, 40
  melon balls à l'orange, 39
Caper sauce, salmon steaks with, 150-151
Caramel-pecan rolls, 191-192
Caraway, Muenster-cheese omelet filling with, 66
Cardamom, poached plums with, 46-47
Caviar, red, and sour-cream omelet filling, 65
Champagne punch bowl, 26

Cheddar-cheese sauce, 70
Cheese
  blintz filling, 94-95
  bread, 183-184
  and ham omelet, 63-64
  and oyster pie, 148
  sauce, 87-88
    corn-ham frittata with, 87
  -stuffed baked tomatoes, 173
  See also names of cheese
Cherry(ies)
  blintz filling, 95
  general data on, 29
  preserves, puffy omelet with, 67
Chicken
  breasts, Benedict, 119-120
  crêpes, curried, 96-97
  curry, 120-121
  curried, salad mold, 121-122
  livers
    en brochette, 118
    chasseur, 118-119
    French omelet with, 62
    omelet filling with mushrooms, 66-67
  in patty shells, 124
  poached, en gelée, 122-123
  soufflé Hollandaise, 70-71
  squab, à la grecque, 124-125
  supreme
    mushrooms and, 127
    vol-au-vent with mushrooms and, 125-127
Chipped beef, creamed, over toasted English muffins, 108
Chive(s)
  cottage-cheese omelet with, 61-62
  -lemon-butter sauce, scallops with, 152
Chocolate
  glaze, 205
  -peppermint milk, 12
Cider, hot mulled, 12-13
Cinnamon
  butter, 180
  oranges with, 41
Clams oregano, 136
Cocoa breakfast crescents, 189-190
Codfish cakes, 137
Coffee
  café brûlot, 17-18

Notes

Notes